CAN ASIANS THINK?

-> Harvard

=> Centre for
Puper national
Affairs

CAN ASIANS THINK?

KISHORE MAHBUBANI

With best wishes,

Kishore

New York Dec '03

TIMES BOOKS INTERNATIONAL
Singapore • Kuala Lumpur

The views expressed in this book are the
personal views of Kishore Mahbubani and
do not in any way represent the views of the
Singapore government.

The author would like to thank the *National
Interest*, *Foreign Affairs*, *Foreign Policy*,
Survival and Peter Van Ness for permission
to reprint the articles in this volume.

Cover photograph of the author at the
7th International Conference on Thinking,
Singapore, June 1997, by courtesy of
The Sunday Times/George Gascon.

© 1998 Times Editions Pte Ltd

Reprinted 1999

Published by Times Editions Pte Ltd
Times Centre
1 New Industrial Road
Singapore 536196
Fax: (65) 2854871 Tel: (65) 2848844
e-mail: te@corp.tpl.com.sg
Online bookstore:
http://www.timesone.com.sg/te

Times Subang
Lot 46, Subang Hi-Tech Industrial Park
Batu Tiga
40000 Shah Alam
Selangor Darul Ehsan
Malaysia
Fax & Tel: (603) 7363517

ISBN 981 204 968 1

In memory of my mother,
Janki Mahbubani

CONTENTS

PREFACE

Can Asians think? Judging from the record of Asian societies over the past few centuries, the answer should be "no"—or, at best, not very well. Several centuries after Portugal burst out of its tiny seams to create colonies all around the world, from Brazil to Angola, from Mozambique to Goa, from Malacca to Macau, Asian societies continued to remain in stupor or stagnation, unaware that European civilisations—which had developed more or less on a par with Asian civilisations until the 15th century or so—had made a great leap forward. Societies that take centuries to wake up cannot be said to think very well. It would be foolish for any Asian to deny this painful historical fact.

By the end of the 20th century (500 years after Portugal made its great leap outwards), it appeared that a few other East Asian societies would follow Japan's lead and become as developed as contemporary Western societies. Then, in a painful repetition of Asian history, they stumbled once again. In early 1998 (when this preface is being written) it is a little too early to tell how serious this stumble is. But having stumbled so often in their efforts to catch up with the West, Asians have an obligation to think—and think very deeply—about their prospects in the coming century and the new millennium. One key purpose of these essays is to stimulate Asian minds to address questions about their future. The lead essay, from which this volume takes its title, is intended for Asian minds. Its key message to Asians is simple: do not think that you have arrived. The rapid economic advances enjoyed by several East Asian societies may, in retrospect, have been the easy part. Retooling the social, political and philosophical dimensions of their societies will be a tougher challenge. This challenge has arrived.

The other essays in this volume are intended for a larger audience. Almost immediately after the end of the Cold War, a mood of triumphalism engulfed Western capitals. Communism had failed. The West had won. Mankind had realised "the end of history". Henceforth, all societies all around the globe, whatever their stage of social and economic development, would become replicas of liberal democratic societies found in the West. The export of democracy from the West to the Rest was seen as an unmitigated good. However, as Robert Kaplan noted in the *Atlantic Monthly* (December 1997), the results of this global export of democracy have been less than ideal:

> The demise of the Soviet Union was no reason for us to pressure Rwanda and other countries to form political parties—though that is what our post-Cold War foreign policy has been largely about, even in parts of the world that the Cold War barely touched. The Eastern European countries liberated in 1989 already had, in varying degrees, the historical and social preconditions for both democracy and advanced industrial life: bourgeois traditions, exposure to the Western Enlightenment, high literacy rates, low birth rates, and so on. The post-Cold War effort to bring democracy to those countries has been reasonable. What is less reasonable is to put a gun to the head of the peoples of the developing world and say, in effect, "Behave as if you had experienced the Western Enlightenment to the degree that Poland and the Czech Republic did. Behave as if 95 percent of your population were literate. Behave as if you had no bloody ethnic or regional disputes."

By late 1997 (eight years after the end of the Cold War), when the hubris arising from the triumph over the Soviet Union had died out, it became possible for some brave souls, such as Robert Kaplan and Fareed Zakaria,[1] to question the value and outcome of the immediate post-Cold War effort to export democracy. In the early 1990s, however, when some of these essays were written, there was no space in the Western intellectual firmament for fundamental questions to be raised about the export of democracy.

I can make this point with some conviction because of several personal encounters I had with Western intellectuals in that period, from Williamsburg to Brussels, from Harvard to Ditchley. In many of these encounters, I was put in the difficult position of being the sole dissenting voice to challenge the conventional wisdom of Western liberals in their moment of triumph. My experience was not unique. Several of my Asian friends confirmed similar experiences. The paradox here was that Western liberal orthodoxy claimed that it celebrated dissenting voices. My personal experience suggested that such tolerance of dissent did not easily extend to challenges of the key intellectual assumptions of this liberal orthodoxy.

These personal encounters convinced me that there was a need to articulate an alternative point of view. My first printed response to the post-Cold War Western hubris was published in the *National Interest* in summer 1992 in an essay entitled "The West and the Rest" (and here I must record my indebtedness to the magazine's editor, Owen Harries, for suggesting this catchy title).

This essay was followed by "Go East, Young Man", published in the *Washington Quarterly* in spring 1994. It gained equal notoriety as "The West and the Rest". "Go East, Young Man" was adapted from a paper entitled "Perspectives on Political Development and the Nature of the Democratic Process: Human Rights and Freedom of the Press", which I delivered at the Asia Society's conference on "Asian and American Perspectives on Capitalism and Democracy" in January 1993.[2] This paper probably contains my sharpest critique of liberal orthodoxy. I have, therefore, decided to republish the full version here.

"Go East, Young Man" was followed by "Pol Pot: The Paradox of Moral Correctness" and "The Dangers of Decadence: What the Rest

Can Teach the West", which was a response to the famous essay "The Clash of Civilizations?" by Samuel Huntington. It was my good fortune that Huntington decided to publish his essay in summer 1993. My responses to his essay seemed to travel almost as widely as his original essay. In the world of writing and publishing, it helps to be read and noticed.

These essays that I published in the early 1990s, together with essays in a similar vein published by other Asians, helped to open a small new chapter in intellectual history. This chapter became known in popular parlance as the "Asian values debate".

The term in itself showed a major misperception in Western minds of the message that Asian voices were putting across in the early 1990s. Many in the West assumed that those who challenged the then contemporary Western ideas in social and political theory were advocating the superiority of Asian values. Actually, the only point that most Asians were trying to make was that Asian values were not inferior. They were trying to say that there was a need for a level playing field in the new intellectual debate of the 1990s. With the advantage of historical hindsight, we can now look at those years and see that Asians were not marching out in that period to proselytise to the West. They were only reacting to Western proselytisation.

One of the key flaws of the campaign to export Western values at the end of the Cold War was the assumption that the good intentions of the West in doing so would lead to good results. This is why in my essay on Pol Pot, I quoted Max Weber as saying: "it is *not* true that good can only follow from good and evil only from evil, but that often the opposite is true. Anyone who says this is, indeed, a political infant."[3] The moral complexity of transporting values from one society or civilisation to another had been lost in the moral certitudes of Western intellectuals at the end of the Cold War. But this moral complexity had been recognised by earlier generations of Western intellectuals. As Reinhold Niebuhr said:

The same strength which has extended our power beyond a continent has also ... brought us into a vast web of history in which other wills, running in oblique or contrasting directions to our own, inevitably hinder or contradict what we most fervently desire. We cannot simply have our way, not even when we believe our way to have the "happiness of mankind" as its promise.

As we approach the end of the 1990s, it is clear that the Asian values debate has subsided. Both sides have retreated from the debate with a sense of embarrassment that each side may have overstated its case. On the Asian side, after the spectacular stumble of several hitherto dynamic East Asian economies, there is a genuine hint of regret at having spoken so confidently of the rise of Asia. Hence, I was not surprised that many of my close friends tried to discourage me from republishing this collection of essays at this unfortunate juncture. The timing did not seem particularly propitious.

But these essays are not intended for any short-term ends. It is only a matter of time (i.e., when, not if) until Asian civilisations reach the same level of development as Western civilisations. The major new reality in East Asia is the genuine conviction and confidence among new Asian minds that their day is coming, even if they have to stumble once or twice more before they make it. Many Asian minds have now been exposed to the highest levels of Western civilisation, in the fields of science and technology, business and administration, arts and literature. Most have clearly thrived at these levels. The Asian mind, having been awakened, cannot be put to sleep in the near future. A new discourse will begin between East and West when Asian societies start to successfully develop again.

When this discourse begins, they will look back at the Asian values debate of the 1990s as only the initial round of a discourse that will last for several centuries. At various points in the history of the past few centuries, when the West experienced its many ascendant moments—either during the peak of the colonial era or in the post-

Cold War period—there developed a conceit that eventually all of mankind would be absorbed into the fabric of Western civilisation. V.S. Naipaul, an Asian child of the West, captured this spirit forcefully when he spoke of Western civilisation as being the only universal civilisation. Indeed, for most of the past few centuries, any other prospect seemed literally inconceivable. The main historical contribution of the ineptly named Asian values debate may have been to call attention to the possibility that other civilisations may yet make equal contributions as Western civilisation to the development and growth of mankind. This is one key reason why this volume of essays is being printed. To ensure an accurate historical record, all the essays are reprinted in full. Thus, the reader may encounter repetitions of certain key arguments.

Having been born a British subject in Singapore and having saluted the British flag as a child, I have had the good fortune of personally experiencing a flow of history that clearly demonstrated that all nations have their ebb and flow. History never stops (or ends). In this shrinking globe of ours, as East and West come closer together, many ancient civilisations will rub together in a direct fashion never seen before in the history of man.

It would be foolish to forecast the outcome of this close rubbing of civilisations. Huntington's vision of a clash of civilisations, frightening though it sounds, needs to be taken seriously. But again, as someone who has had the good fortune to experience the rise of the Asia-Pacific era, I remain absolutely convinced that the future lies in the fusion of civilisations. This is the vision I tried to portray in a lecture I delivered at the IISS (International Institute of Strategic Studies) annual meeting in Vancouver in September 1994. *Survival*, the IISS journal, printed an edited version of this lecture in an article entitled "The Pacific Impulse", which is republished here.

Over the course of the past few years, I have also published essays on various other topics. Some of these are republished in this volume. Given my conviction that the centre of gravity of the world's economy will rest firmly in the Asia-Pacific region, I have written several essays on various aspects of the region. Hence, I am also reprinting "Japan Adrift" (written in Harvard), "An Asia-Pacific Consensus" and "Seven Paradoxes on Asia-Pacific Security".

I published my first essay in *Foreign Affairs* 15 years ago on the Cambodian question. I am not republishing it here as that particular chapter of Cambodian history has closed. In the course of the decade-long debate on Cambodia, which became a modern metaphor for tragedy during Pol Pot's rule, I encountered another unusual strand in the Western mind: the desire to believe that there were black and white solutions for complex moral issues. It was in response to this that I wrote the essay "Pol Pot: The Paradox of Moral Correctness".

I have also been a student of Southeast Asia. It has been a miracle of history that this region (which has greater diversity of race, language, religion, culture, etc., than the Balkans of Europe) has emerged as one of the most peaceful and prosperous corners of the world. This modern miracle is little understood. To explain it to the Japanese audience, I wrote an essay entitled "The ASEAN Magic", which was published in the official journal of Japan's Ministry of Foreign Affairs.

Since I am a Singaporean, this volume would be incomplete if I did not include an essay on my own country. I have had the good fortune of being a citizen of one of the most successful developing countries of the world. Despite Singapore's success, it has had the occasional misfortune of suffering bad press that gives no due recognition to the very special achievements the country has had in economic and social development. Hence, when the UNDP asked me to write a short essay on Singapore's developmental experience, I was happy to do so.

Finally, in keeping with the spirit of many of these essays, I have decided to end on a provocative note by republishing "The Ten Commandments for Developing Countries in the Nineties". These 10 commandments were written for a UNDP conference on development, but they were reprinted and republished in English, French and

German. Brevity, I have learned, is universally appreciated. Hence, I will end my preface here and let the essays tell the rest of the story.

---

1. Fareed Zakaria, "The Rise of Illiberal Democracy", *Foreign Affairs*, November/December 1997.
2. James Fallows was my fellow panellist at this seminar, and judging from his response, it would be fair to say that he was shocked by this essay.
3. Max Weber, *Politics As a Vocation*, Philadelphia, Fortress Press, 1965, p. 49.

———

CAN ASIANS THINK?

——

EDITED AND UPDATED VERSION OF A LECTURE THE AUTHOR DELIVERED AT
THE 7TH INTERNATIONAL CONFERENCE ON THINKING IN SINGAPORE
ON 3 JUNE 1997. *NATIONAL INTEREST*, SUMMER 1998.

The 7th International Conference on Thinking was held
in Singapore in June 1997. It needed some Asian voices.
When I was asked to speak, one question immediately
popped into my mind: "Can Asians think as well as others?"
The answer, I discovered, was a complex one. This lecture
represents my first stab at the question. The key purpose
is to launch a debate among Asian minds. But I wonder
whether people from other continents may wish to ask
similar questions, such as "Can Europeans think?" or "Can
Americans think?" Following is an updated version of this
lecture, published in the form of an essay in the *National
Interest* in summer 1998.

Can Asians think? This is obviously a sensitive question. In this age of political correctness that we live in, just imagine the uproar that could be caused if I went to Europe or Africa and posed the question "Can Europeans think?" or "Can Africans think?" You have to be Asian to ask the question "Can Asians think?"

Given its sensitivity, let me explain both the reasons why and the context in which I am posing the question. First, if you had to ask one single, key question that could determine the future of the globe, it may well be "Can Asians think?" In 1996 Asians already made up 3.5 billion out of a global population of over 5 billion (or about 70 percent of the world population). By conservative projections, the Asian portion of the world population will increase to 5.7 billion in 2050 out of a global population of 9.87 billion, while the populations of North America and Europe will remain relatively constant at 374 million and 721 million respectively. Clearly, in the past few centuries Europe and, more recently, North America have carried the larger share of the global burden in advancing human civilisation. By 2050, when Europeans and North Americans make up one-tenth instead of one-sixth of the world's population, would it be fair for the remaining 90 percent of mankind to expect this 10 percent to continue to bear this burden? Realistically, can the rest of the world continue to rest on the shoulders of the West? If Asians double in population in the next 50 years, will they be able to carry their fair share of this burden?

Second, I am not asking this question about individual Asians in terms of limited thinking abilities. Clearly, Asians can master alphabets, add two plus two to make four, and play chess. However, throughout history, there have been examples of societies that have produced brilliant individuals yet experienced a lot of grief collectively. The classic example of this is Jewish society. Per capita, Jews have contributed more brilliant minds, from Einstein to Wittgenstein, from Disraeli to Kissinger, than any other society. Yet, as a society they have suffered greatly, especially in the past century or so. Let me stress that I am not speaking about the travails of Israel in modern times. I am speaking of the period from A.D. 135, when the Jews were forced to leave Palestine, to 1948, when Israel was born. Will a similar fate befall Asian societies, or will they be able to think well and ensure a better future for themselves?

Third, the time scale in which I am posing this question is not in terms of days, weeks, months, years or even decades. I am looking at the question from the time scale of centuries, especially since we stand two years away from the new millennium. Arguably, the future course of world history in the next few centuries, as I will explain later, will depend on how Asian societies think and perform.

Back to the question "Can Asians think?" In a multiple-choice examination format, there would be three possible answers to the question: "Yes", "No" or "Maybe". Before we decide which choice to tick, let me make a case for each answer.

NO, THEY CANNOT THINK

I will start with the reasons for the "No" answer, if only to refute any critics who may suggest that the question itself is manifestly absurd. If one looks at the record of the past thousand years, one can make a very persuasive case that Asians, Asian societies that is, cannot think.

Let us look at where Asian societies were 1,000 years ago, say in the year 997. Then, the Chinese and the Arabs (i.e., Confucian and Islamic civilisations) led the way in science and technology, medicine and astronomy. The Arabs adopted both the decimal system and the numbers 0 to 9 from India, and they learned how to make paper from the Chinese. The world's first university was founded just over 1,000 years ago, in the year 971, in Cairo. By contrast, Europe was then still in what has been described as the "Dark Ages", which had begun when the Roman Empire collapsed in the fifth century. As Will Durant puts it in *The Age of Faith*:

Western Europe in the sixth century was a chaos of conquest, disintegration, and rebarbarization. Much of the classic culture survived, for the most part silent and hidden in a few monasteries and families. But the physical and psychological foundations of social order had been so disturbed that centuries would be needed to restore them. Love of letters, devotion to art, the unity and continuity of culture, the cross-fertilization of communicating minds, fell before the convulsions of war, the perils of transport, the economies of poverty, the rise of vernaculars, the disappearance of Latin from the East and of Greek from the West.[1]

Against this backdrop, it would have been sheer folly to predict at the time that in the second millennium Chinese, Indian and Islamic civilisations would slip into the backwaters of history while Europe would rise to be the first civilisation ever to dominate the entire globe. But that, of course, is precisely what happened.

It did not come about suddenly. Until about the 16th century, the more advanced societies of Asia, while they had lost their primacy, were still on a par with those of Europe and there was no definite indication that Europe would leap far ahead. At that time, Europe's relative weaknesses were more apparent than its strengths. It was not the most fertile area of the world, nor was it particularly populous—important criteria by the measure of the day, when the soil was the source of most wealth, and human and animal muscle of most power. Europe exhibited no pronounced advantages in the fields of culture, mathematics, or engineering, navigation or other technologies. It was also a deeply fragmented continent, consisting of a hodgepodge of petty kingdoms, principalities and city-states. Further, at the end of the 15th century, Europe was in the throes of a bloody conflict with the mighty Ottoman Empire, which was pushing its way, inexorably it seemed, towards the gates of Vienna. So perduring was this threat that German princes hundreds of kilometres from the front lines had got into the custom of sending tribute—*Turkenverehrung*—to the Sublime Porte in Istanbul.

Asian cultures, on the other hand, appeared to be thriving in the 15th century. China, for example, had a highly developed and vibrant culture. Its unified, hierarchic administration was run by well-educated Confucian bureaucrats who had given a coherence and sophistication to Chinese society that was unparalleled. China's technological prowess was also formidable. Printing by movable type had already appeared in the 11th century. Paper money had expedited the flow of commerce and growth of markets. China's gargantuan iron industry, coupled with the invention of gunpowder, gave it immense military strength.

However, almost amazingly, it was Europe that leapt ahead. Something almost magical happened to European minds, and this was followed by wave after wave of progress and advance of civilisations, from the Renaissance to the Enlightenment, from the scientific revolution to the industrial revolution. While Asian societies degenerated into backwardness and ossification, European societies, propelled forward by new forms of economic organisation, military-technical dynamism, political pluralism within the continent as a whole (if not within all individual countries), and the uneven beginnings of intellectual liberty, notably in Italy, Britain and Holland, produced what would have been called at the time the "European miracle"—had there been an observing, superior civilisation to mark the event. Because that mix of critical ingredients did not exist in any of the Asian societies, they appeared to stand still while Europe advanced to the centre of the world stage. Colonisation, which began in the 16th century, and the industrial revolution in the 19th century, augmented and entrenched Europe's dominant position.

To me, coming from Singapore, with a population of 3 million, it is a source of great wonder that a small state like Portugal, also with a population of a few million, could carve out territories like Goa, Macau and Malacca from larger and more ancient civilisations. It was an amazing feat. But what is more amazing is that it was done in the 1500s. The Portuguese colonisers were followed by the Spanish, the Dutch, the French, then the British. Throughout this period, for almost three centuries or more, Asian societies lay prostrate and allowed themselves to be surpassed and colonised by far smaller societies.

The most painful thing that happened to Asia was not the physical but the mental colonisation. Many Asians (including, I fear, many of my ancestors from South Asia) began to believe that Asians were inferior beings to the Europeans. Only this could explain how a few thousand British could control a few hundred million people in South Asia. If I am allowed to make a controversial point here, I would add that this mental colonisation has not been completely eradicated in Asia, and many Asian societies are still struggling to break free.

It is truly astonishing that even today, as we stand on the eve of the 21st century, 500 years after the arrival of the first Portuguese colonisers in Asia, only one—I repeat, one—Asian society has reached, in a comprehensive sense, the level of development that prevails generally in Europe and North America today. The Japanese mind was the first to be awakened in Asia, beginning with the Meiji Restoration in the 1860s. Japan was first considered developed and more or less accepted as an equal by 1902, when it signed the Anglo-Japanese alliance.

If Asian minds can think, why is there today only one Asian society able to catch up with the West? I rest my case for the negative answer to our question. Those of you who want to tick "No" to the question "Can Asians think?" can proceed to do so.

YES, THEY CAN

Let me now try to draw out the arguments why we might answer "Yes" to the question "Can Asians think?"

The first, and the most obvious one, is the incredible economic performance of East Asian societies in the past few decades. Japan's success, while it has not been fully replicated in the rest of Asia, has set off ripples that now, current problems notwithstanding, have the potential to become tidal waves. Japan's economic success was first followed by the emergence of the "four tigers" (South Korea, Taiwan, Hong Kong and Singapore). But the success of these four tigers convinced other Southeast Asian countries, especially Indonesia,

Malaysia and Thailand, that they could do the same. Lately they have been followed by China, which now has the potential to overtake the United States and become the world's largest economy by 2020. What is amazing is the pace of economic development. It took the British 58 years (from 1780), America 47 years (from 1839) and Japan 33 years (from the 1880s) to double their economic output. On the other hand, it took Indonesia 17 years, South Korea 11 years and China 10 years to do the same. As a whole, the East Asian miracle economies grew more rapidly and more consistently than any other group of economies in the world from 1960 to 1990. They averaged 5.5 percent annual per capita real income growth, outperforming every economy in Latin America and Sub-Saharan Africa and even the OECD economies, which averaged only 2.5 percent growth in that period.

You cannot get good grades in an examination by luck. It requires intelligence and hard work. Similarly, you cannot get good economic performance, especially of the scale seen in Asia, simply by luck. It reflects both intelligence and hard work. And it is vital to stress here that the pace and scale of the economic explosion seen in Asia is unprecedented in the history of man. The chief economist of the World Bank, Joseph Stiglitz, captured this reality well in his article in the *Asian Wall Street Journal*:

> The East Asian 'miracle' was real. Its economic transformation of East Asia has been one of the most remarkable accomplishments in history. The dramatic surge in gross domestic product which it brought about is reflected in higher standards of living for hundreds of millions of Asians, including longer life expectancy, better health and education, and millions of others have rescued themselves from poverty, and now lead more hopeful lives. These achievements are real, and will be far more permanent than the present turmoil.[2]

The confidence of East Asians has been further boosted by the numerous studies that demonstrate the impressive academic performance of East Asians, both in leading Western universities and at home. Today many of the top students produced by American universities are of Asian origin. Educational excellence is an essential prerequisite for cultural confidence. To put it baldly, many Asians are pleased to wake up to the new realisation that their minds are not inferior. Most Westerners cannot appreciate the change because they can never directly feel the sense of inferiority many Asians experienced until recently.

The second reason why we might answer "Yes" to the question "Can Asians think?" is that a vital switch is taking place in many Asian minds. For centuries, Asians believed that the only way to progress was through emulation of the West. Yukichi Fukuzawa, a leading Meiji reformer, epitomised this attitude when he said in the late 19th century that for Japan to progress, it had to learn from the West. The other leading modernisers in Asia, whether they be Sun Yat-sen or Jawaharlal Nehru, shared this fundamental attitude. The mental switch that is taking place in Asian minds today is that they no longer believe that the only way to progress is through copying; they now believe they can work out their own solutions.

This switch in Asian minds has taken place slowly and imperceptibly. Until a few decades ago, Western societies beckoned as beacons on the hill: living models of the most successful form of human societies—economically prosperous, politically stable, socially just and harmonious, ethically clean, and, all in all, providing environments that had the best possible conditions for their citizens to grow and thrive as individuals. These societies were not perfect, but they were clearly superior, in all senses of the word, to any society outside. Until recently it would have been folly, and indeed inconceivable, for any Asian intellectual to suggest, "This may not be the path we want to take". Today this is what many Asians are thinking, privately if not publicly.

However, overall, there is no question that Western societies remain more successful than their East Asian counterparts. And they retain fields of excellence in areas that no other society comes close to, in their universities, think tanks, and certainly in cultural realms. No Asian orchestra comes close in performance to the leading Western orchestras, even though the musical world in the West has been enriched by many brilliant Asian musicians. But Asians are shocked by the scale and depth of social and economic problems that have afflicted many Western societies. In North America, societies are troubled by the relative breakdown of the family as an institution, the plague of drug addiction and its attendant problems, including crime, the persistence of ghettos and the perception that there has been a decline in ethical standards. This is exemplified by statistics provided by the US government that reflect social trends for the period 1960–90. During that 30-year period, the rate of violent crime quadrupled, single parent families almost tripled, and the number of US state and federal prisoners tripled. Asians are also troubled by the addiction of Europeans to their social security nets despite the clear evidence that these nets now hold down their societies and have created a sense of gloom about long-term economic prospects. In previous decades, when East Asians visited North America and Western Europe, they envied the high standards of living and better quality of life in those societies. Today, though the high standards of living remain in the West, Asians no longer consider these societies as their role models. They are beginning to believe that they can attempt something different.

A simple metaphor may explain what Western minds would see if they could peer into Asian minds. Until recently, most of those minds shared the general assumption that the developmental path of all societies culminated in the plateau on which most Western societies now rest. Hence, all societies, with minor variations, would end up creating liberal, democratic societies, giving emphasis to individual freedoms, as they moved up the socio-economic ladder. Today Asians can still see the plateau of contentment that most Western societies rest on, but they can also see, beyond the plateau, alternative peaks to which they can take their societies. Instead of seeing the plateau as the natural end destination, they now have a desire to bypass it (for they do not wish to be afflicted by some of the social and cultural ills that afflict Western societies) and to search for alternative peaks beyond. This kind of mental horizon never existed in Asian minds until recently. It reveals the new confidence of Asians in themselves.

The third reason why we might answer "Yes" to the question "Can Asians think?" is that today is not the only period when Asian minds have begun to stir. As more and more Asians lift their lives from levels of survival, they have the economic freedom to think, reflect, and rediscover their cultural heritage. There is a growing consciousness that their societies, like those in the West, have a rich social, cultural and philosophical legacy that they can resuscitate and use to evolve their own modern and advanced societies. The richness and depth of Indian and Chinese civilisations, to name just two, have been acknowledged by Western scholars. Indeed, for the past few centuries, it was Western scholarship and endeavour that preserved the fruits of Asian civilisation, just as the Arabs preserved and passed on the Greek and Roman civilisations in the darkest days of Europe. For example, while Asian cultures deteriorated, museums and universities in the West preserved and even cherished the best that Asian art and culture had produced. As Asians delve deeper into their own cultural heritage, they find their minds nourished. For the first time in centuries, an Asian renaissance is under way. Visitors to Asian cities—from Teheran to Calcutta, from Bombay to Shanghai, from Singapore to Hong Kong—now see both a newfound confidence as well as an interest in traditional language and culture. As their economies grow and as they have more disposable income, Asians spend it increasingly on reviving traditional dance or theatre. What we are witnessing today are only the bare beginnings of a major cultural rediscovery. The pride that Asians are taking in their culture is clear and palpable.

In short, Asians who would like to rush and answer "Yes" to the question have more than ample justification for doing so. But before they do so, I would advise them to pause and reflect on the reasons for the "Maybe" answer before arriving at a final judgement.

THE "MAYBE" RESPONSE

Despite the travails sparked by the financial crisis in late 1997, most Asians continue to be optimistic about their future. Such optimism is healthy. Yet it may be useful for Asians to learn a small lesson in history from the experience of Europeans exactly a century ago, when Europe was full of optimism. In his book *Out of Control*, Zbigniew Brzezinski describes how the world looked then:

> The twentieth century was born in hope. It dawned in a relatively benign setting. The principal powers of the world had enjoyed, broadly speaking, a relatively prolonged spell of peace .... The dominant mood in the major capitals as of January 1, 1900, was generally one of optimism. The structure of global power seemed stable. Existing empires appeared to be increasingly enlightened as well as secure.[3]

Despite this great hope, the 20th century became, in Brzezinski's words:

> ... mankind's most bloody and hateful century, a century of hallucinating politics and of monstrous killings. Cruelty was institutionalized to an unprecedented degree, lethality was organized on a mass production basis. The contrast between the scientific potential for good and the political evil that was actually unleashed is shocking. Never before in history was killing so globally pervasive, never before did it consume so many lives, never before was human annihilation pursued with such concentration of sustained effort on behalf of such arrogantly irrational goals.[4]

One of the most important questions that an Asian has to ask himself today is a simple one: Can any Asian society, with the exception of Japan (which is an accepted member of the Western club), be absolutely confident that it can succeed and do as well in a comprehensive sense as contemporary advanced societies in North America and Western Europe? If the answer is none, or even a few, then the case for the "Maybe" response becomes stronger.

There are still many great challenges that Asian societies have to overcome before they can reach the comprehensive level of achievement enjoyed by Western societies. The first challenge in the development of any society is economic. Until the middle of 1997, most East Asian societies believed that they had mastered the basic rules of modern economics. They liberalised their economies, encouraged foreign investment flows and practised thrifty fiscal policies. The high level of domestic savings gave them a comfortable economic buffer. After enjoying continuous economic growth rates of 7 percent or more per annum for decades, it was natural for societies like South Korea, Thailand, Indonesia and Malaysia to assume that they had discovered the magical elixir of economic development.

The events following the devaluation of the Thai baht on 2 July 1997 demonstrated that they had not. The remarkable thing about this financial crisis was that no economist anticipated its depth or scale. Economists and analysts are still divided on its fundamental causes. As the crisis is still unfolding as this essay is being written, it is too early to provide definitive judgements on the fundamental causes. But a few suggestions are worth making.

On the economic front, many mistakes were made. In Thailand, for example, the decision to sustain fixed exchange rates between the baht and the dollar, despite the disparity in interest rates, allowed Thai businessmen to borrow cheap in US dollars and earn high interest rates in Thai baht. This also led to overinvestments in Thailand, in the property and share markets. All this was clearly unsustainable. The IMF provided some discreet warnings. However, the relatively weak coalition governments then prevailing in Thailand were unable to administer the bitter medicine required to remedy the situation because some of it had to be administered to their financial backers.

Domestically, it was a combination of economic and political factors that precipitated and prolonged the financial crisis.

There was also a huge new factor that complicated the story: the force of globalisation. The key lesson that all East Asian economic managers have learned from the 1997–98 crisis is that they are accountable not only to domestic actors but to the international financial markets and their key players. The East Asians should not have been surprised. It was a logical consequence of liberalisation and integration with the global economy. Integration has brought both benefits (in terms of significant increases in standard of living) and costs (such as loss of autonomy in economic management). But there was a clear reluctance to acknowledge and accept the loss of autonomy. This was demonstrated by the state of denial that characterised the initial East Asian response to this crisis. The denial clearly showed the psychological time lag in East Asian minds in facing up to new realities.

Significantly, the two East Asian economies that have (after the initial bouts of denial) swallowed most fully the bitter medicine administered by the IMF have been the two societies that have progressed fastest in developing middle classes that have integrated themselves into the world view of the new interconnected global universe of modern economics. South Korea and Thailand, although they continue to face serious economic challenges at the time of writing, have clearly demonstrated that their elites are now well plugged in to the new financial networks. The new finance minister of Thailand, Tarrin Nimmanhaeminda, walks and talks with ease in any key financial capital. His performance is one indicator of the new globalised Asian mind that is emerging.

The 1997–98 financial crisis also demonstrated the wisdom of the Chinese in translating the English word "crisis" as a combination of two Chinese characters, "danger" and "opportunity". Clearly, East Asian societies have experienced many dangerous moments. But if they emerge from the 1997–98 financial crisis with restructured and reinvigorated economic and administrative systems of management, they may yet be among the first societies in the world to develop strong immune systems to handle present and future challenges springing from globalisation. It is too early to tell whether this is true. And this in turn reinforces the point that on the economic front, one should perhaps give the "Maybe" answer to the question "Can Asians think?"

Second, on the political front, most Asian societies, including East Asian societies, have a long way to go before they can reach Western levels of political stability and harmony. There is little danger of a coup d'état or real civil war in most contemporary Western societies (with the possible exception, still, of Northern Ireland). Western societies have adopted political variations of the liberal democratic model, even though the presidential systems of the United States and France differ significantly from the Westminster models of the United Kingdom, Canada and Australia. These political forms are not perfect. They contain many features that inhibit social progress, from vested interest lobby groups to pork-barrel politics. Indeed, it would be fair to say that political development in most Western societies has atrophied. But it has atrophied at comfortable levels. Most of their citizens live in domestic security, fear no oppression, and are content with their political frameworks. How many Asian societies can claim to share this benign state of affairs? The answer is clearly very few. And if it is equally clear that they are *not* going to enjoy this in the very near future, then this again militates in favour of the "Maybe" answer.

Third, in the security realm, the one great advantage Western societies have over the rest of the world is that war among them has become a thing of the past. The reason for this is complex. It includes an awareness of ethnic affinity among Western tribes who feel outnumbered by the rest of the world's population and also a sense of belonging to a common civilisation. It may also reflect the exhaustion of having fought too many wars in the past. Nevertheless, it is truly remarkable, when we count the number of wars—and truly big wars—

that the English, French and Germans have fought with each other (including two in this century), that there is today almost a zero chance of war between the United Kingdom, France and Germany. This is a remarkably civilised thing to have achieved, reflecting a considerable step forward in the history of human civilisation. When will India and Pakistan, or North and South Korea, achieve this same zero prospect of war? And if the answer is not in the near future, is it reasonable to suggest that perhaps Asian minds (or the minds of Asian societies) have not reached the same level as the West?

Fourth, Asians face serious challenges in the social realm. While it is true that it took the social dislocations caused by the industrial revolution to eradicate the feudal traces of European cultures (social freedom followed economic freedom), it is still unclear whether similar economic revolutions in East Asia will have the same liberating social effects on Asian societies. Unfortunately, many feudal traces, especially those of clannishness and nepotism, continue to prevent Asian societies from becoming truly meritocratic ones, where individual citizens are able to grow and thrive on the basis of their abilities and not on the basis of their birth or connections or ethnic background.

Fifth and finally, and perhaps most fundamentally, the key question remains whether Asian minds will be able to develop the right blend of values that will both preserve some of the traditional strengths of Asian values (e.g., attachment to the family as an institution, deference to societal interests, thrift, conservatism in social mores, respect for authority) as well as absorb the strengths of Western values (the emphasis on individual achievement, political and economic freedom, respect for the rule of law as well as for key national institutions). This will be a complex challenge.

One of the early (and perhaps inevitable) reactions by some Western commentators to the 1997–98 financial crisis was to suggest that it fundamentally reflected the failure of Asian values. If nothing else, this quick reaction suggested that the "Asian values debate" of the early 1990s had touched some sensitive nerves in the Western mind and soul. The desire to bury Asian values revealed the real pain that had been inflicted during that debate.

The true test of the viability and validity of values is shown not in theory but in practice. Those who try to draw a direct link of causality between adherence to Asian values and financial disaster have a tough empirical case to make because of the varied reactions of East Asian societies to the financial crisis. South Korea and Thailand, two of the three countries that were most deeply affected by the crisis (i.e., those who had to turn to the IMF for assistance), had been given the highest marks in Western minds for their moves towards democratisation. The three open economies that were least affected by the financial crisis were Taiwan, Hong Kong and Singapore, and the three had very different political systems. In short, there was no clear correlation between political systems and financial vulnerability.

The only correlation that is clear so far is that between good governance and resilience in the financial crisis. Good governance is not associated with any single political system or ideology. It is associated with the willingness and ability of the government to develop economic, social and administrative systems that are resilient enough to handle the challenges brought about in the new economic era we are moving into. China provides a good living example of this. Its leaders are not looking for the perfect political system in theory. They are searching daily for pragmatic solutions to keep their society moving forward. The population support this pragmatism, for they too feel that it is time for China to catch up. Traditionally, the Chinese have looked for good government, not minimal government. They can recognise good governance when they experience it. The fact that Japan—which is in Western eyes the most liberal and democratic East Asian society—has had great difficulties adapting to the new economic environment demonstrates that political openness is not the key variable to look at.

It is vital for Western minds to understand that the efforts by Asians to rediscover Asian values are not only, or even primarily, a search for political values. Instead, they represent a complex set of motives and aspirations in Asian minds: a desire to reconnect with their historical past after this connection had been ruptured both by colonial rule and by the subsequent domination of the globe by a Western *Weltanschauung*; an effort to find the right balance in bringing up their young so that they are open to the new technologically interconnected global universe and yet rooted in and conscious of the cultures of their ancestors; an effort to define their own personal, social and national identities in a way that enhances their sense of self-esteem in a world where their immediate ancestors had subconsciously accepted that they were lesser beings in a Western universe. In short, the reassertion of Asian values in the 1990s represents a complex process of regeneration and rediscovery that is an inevitable aspect of the rebirth of societies.

Here again, it is far too early to tell whether Asian societies can successfully both integrate themselves into the modern world and reconnect with their past. Both are mammoth challenges. Western minds have a clear advantage over Asian minds, as they are convinced that their successful leap into modernity was to a large extent a result of the compatibility of their value systems with the modern universe. Indeed, many Western minds believe (consciously or subconsciously) that without Western value systems no society can truly enter the modern universe.

Only time will tell whether Asian societies can enter the modern universe as Asian societies rather than Western replicas. Since it is far too early to pass judgement on whether they will succeed in this effort, it is perhaps fair to suggest that this too is another argument in favour of the "Maybe" answer to the question "Can Asians think?"

CONCLUSION

Clearly, the 21st century and the next millennium will prove to be very challenging for Asian societies. For most of the past 500 years, they have fallen behind European societies in many different ways.

There is a strong desire to catch up. The real answer to the question "Can Asians think?" will be provided if they do so. Until then, Asians will do themselves a big favour by constantly reminding themselves why this question remains a valid one for them to pose to themselves. And only they can answer it. No one else can.

1. Will Durant, *The Age of Faith*, New York, Simon & Schuster, 1950, p. 450.
2. Joseph Stiglitz, *The Asian Wall Street Journal,* 2 February 1998.
3. Zbigniew Brzezinski, *Out of Control*, New York, Charles Scribner's Sons, 1993, p. 3.
4. Ibid, pp. 4–5.

ASIAN VALUES

THE WEST AND THE REST

THE NATIONAL INTEREST, NUMBER 28, SUMMER 1992.

My year at Harvard, from September 1991 to June 1992, opened my eyes in many ways. One key insight I gained was that those who live and think in the West are not aware of how they impact on the rest of the world or how the Rest thinks of the West. The Western mind believes that it understands all worlds, since it is open to all ideas and closed to none. The paradoxical result of this deep-seated assumption is that the Western mind is actually unaware of the limits of its understanding and comprehension. This essay was an attempt to open new windows in the Western mind.

The West won the Cold War, the conventional wisdom holds, not because of its military superiority but because of the strength of its social, economic and political institutions. Hence, it is not surprising that a new consensus has quickly developed that the West merely has to hold a steady course in the post-Cold War era. Francis Fukuyama, with his celebration of the triumph of Western values, captured the spirit of the moment. The rest of the world, if it is to free itself from the "mire" of history, will have to adjust and accommodate to the ways of the West. Having already got things basically right and facing no imminent threat, the West has no need to make major adjustments of its own.

This essay will challenge these widely held assumptions. It will argue that "steady as she goes" is not a viable option for the West; that while it may not face any immediate military threat, the West faces serious and growing dangers of other kinds; that it cannot afford to turn its back on the Third World because the Cold War is over; that in a shrinking and increasingly overcrowded world, in which the population of the West constitutes an ever smaller percentage, a comprehensive new strategy is needed; and that an aggressive effort to export Western values to the non-West does not constitute such a strategy, but will only serve to aggravate already serious problems.

Arriving at a sound strategy, a difficult enough task in the best of circumstances, will be harder because of the deeply ingrained habits acquired during the long years of the Cold War. There is a real danger that problems will be wrongly identified and defined, and that consequently the West's strategic sights will be pointed the wrong way. For someone of my background, this danger recalls the famous British guns of Singapore in December 1941. The guns of that supposedly impregnable fortress were confidently pointed seaward, as the Japanese came quietly over land on bicycles and on foot to conquer the island with embarrassing ease. This analogy is particularly apt because one of the most serious challenges that will confront the West in the new era will also arrive on bicycles and on foot, or their equivalents: the challenge posed by mass immigration from Third World countries. Superior Western military technology will be useless against these invading armies because they will arrive as poor and defenceless individuals and families, moving without commanders or orders, and seeping slowly through porous borders.

If and when this happens, it will be only one dimension of a multiple crisis, a crisis resulting from the combination of a fundamentally changed Western attitude towards the Third World, and some well-known but inadequately understood secular trends.

THE RETREAT OF THE WEST

For the four decades of the Cold War, both sides attached great importance to the Third World. Seeing themselves as engaged in a global struggle for the highest stakes, neither felt able to treat any country, however small, poor or distant, as unimportant. Everything counted; nothing was irrelevant. Even as the West shed its colonial empires, the Third World successor states became more rather than less strategically relevant, especially for the United States. Because everyone else was already committed to one camp or the other, these countries constituted the main arena of competition, the contested hearts and minds and territories of the Cold War.

Although most Third World countries belonged at least nominally to the Non-Aligned Movement, that organisation was incapable of providing them with effective security. For that, most felt they had only two effective choices: to identify to a greater or lesser degree with either the Western or Soviet camp. Thus a ramifying system of patrons and clients, one with an elaborate if mostly tacit set of rules, spread over the globe. Third World states were by no means always the passive objects of superpower manipulation in these arrangements, and many became very skilful at exploiting the Cold War for their own ends. But it was a dangerous game, requiring precise calculation. Those playing it observed carefully what happened to countries like Cambodia and Ethiopia—two vivid symbols of 20th-century tragedy—

when they got things wrong. They also noticed that if the Soviets kept Mengistu in power in Ethiopia, the West kept Mobutu in Zaire. This was a time when strategic imperatives did not allow for exquisite moral scrupulousness.

With the end of the Cold War, this state of affairs no longer pertains. Following the disappearance of the Soviet Union, Soviet proxies have either already fallen (like Mengistu) or been left exposed, without protection or subsidies, at the end of a long limb. The West, too, has reordered its priorities. No longer is there the same compulsion to prop up unsavoury allies, in the name of national security. More stringent tests of human rights and democratic rectitude can be applied, and the inability of such allies to transform themselves at short notice to comply with these higher standards has been used as justification for abandoning some of them without feeling much in the way of guilt.

Whatever the ethical merits of thus using and then ditching allies, this sudden joint Soviet and Western abandonment of their erstwhile Third World friends has sent a powerful message through most of the Third World. The rules of the game have changed; indeed, the game itself has changed. Third World regimes have begun to realise that their previous "usefulness" has ended and the West now sees little value in taking any real interest in their fate. The results of this are not all bad. The end of superpower competition has created the conditions for the ending of many conflicts that were kept well-stoked by the Cold War, ranging from El Salvador through Namibia and Afghanistan to Cambodia. Many dictatorial regimes have disappeared. This is to be welcomed. But the removal of Cold War pressures also means that forces that have been bottled up in these societies can now erupt.

To understand the epochal significance of this new Western tendency to withdraw and leave most Third World societies alone (observe, for example, how many Western embassies are closing down in Africa; the British have in recent years closed their missions in Burundi, Congo, Gabon, Liberia and Somalia), consider that these societies have been subjected to heavy Western involvement in their affairs since the colonial era started in the 16th century. The current Western tendency to disentangle itself from the Third World should therefore be seen as the end not merely of a four-decades-old involvement, but of one that is four centuries old. All the indigenous processes that were smothered and subdued for centuries, either because of metropolitan pressures or because global forces were raging above them, can finally surface. To hold these historically pent-up forces in place, the Western world has left behind in the Third World a thin veneer of Western concepts of national sovereignty, the nation-state, sometimes Western parliamentary institutions, and some principles of international law.

True, these forces were not totally bottled up during the Cold War. But the end of that struggle has already seen an acceleration and intensification of such phenomena that amount to a qualitative change. Tribal warfare in Africa, ethnic strife in Pakistan, Hindu-Muslim strife in India, Islamic fundamentalism in Algeria: all can surface now with greater strength. The disintegration in 1991 of Somalia (one of the more ethnically homogeneous states in Africa) would not have been viewed with indifference—would not have been allowed to happen—10 years ago. During the Cold War, the main political fault lines in South Asia were *between* India and Pakistan, fault lines accentuated by their superpower patrons. Today, the main fault lines are inside India and Pakistan.

THE SHRINKING GLOBE
In short, the reversal of centuries-old Western processes of intervention in the Third World is probably going to lead to the emergence of a cauldron of instability in most of the Third World. In previous centuries geographic distance would have insulated the West from this cauldron. Ironically, it was during the Cold War that Western technology shrank the world into a global village, destroying the insulation provided by distance and time.

Global communication networks that give the West a ringside seat when a Tiananmen explodes or a Gulf War breaks out have an equally spectacular reverse effect. Increasingly, once-remote villages in China, Central Asia and the heart of Africa now have clear pictures of the comfortable and affluent lives of ordinary citizens in the West. Clausewitz once observed that "once barriers—which in a sense consist only in man's ignorance of the possible—are torn down, they are not easily set up again." It is a remark worth bearing in mind in this context.

The simple practical effect of all this is that a single mental universe and a single global society are in the process of being created. All through the early and middle decades of the 20th century, Western societies had to struggle hard to remove from themselves the gross inequalities resulting from the early years of industrialisation. This they essentially did. Now they are faced with a much, much larger proletariat on their doorsteps—one drawn irresistibly by awareness of Western affluence and opportunity.

Western Europeans are beginning to understand this. If something goes wrong in, say, Algeria or Tunisia, the problems will impact on France. In the eyes of the North African population, the Mediterranean, which once divided civilisations, has become a mere pond. What human being would not cross a pond if thereby he could improve his livelihood? Through all previous centuries, men and women have crossed oceans and mountains to seek a better life, often suffering terrible hardship in the process. Indeed, it is this drive that explains the wide geographic span of "Western" societies outside their origins in continental Europe, stretching from North America through South Africa to Australia and New Zealand. Today, many more people feel that they can make similar journeys. So far, Western Europeans have only seen the beginnings of such mass movements, and already they are deeply troubled.

In 1990, the ratio of Europe's population to that of Africa was 498 million to 642 million; according to UN projections, by 2050, based on medium fertility extension, the ratio will be 486 million (a decrease, be it noted) to 2.265 billion—that is, a ratio akin to the white-black ratio in today's South Africa. Two nations, currently of the same population size, demonstrate the meaning of this trend. In the past few years, despite net immigration, Italy's population has been declining. Egypt's is growing by a million every eight months. Italy reacted very harshly to the Albanian boat people. How much more harshly would it react if the boat people were not fellow Europeans? Or consider this: In 1960, the combined population of Morocco and Algeria amounted to half that of France; today it is about equal; in another 30 years it will be double that of France.

To put it simply, within a few decades, when Western Europe will be confronted with teeming impoverished masses on its borders and when increasing numbers will be slipping in to join the millions already there, Europeans will find themselves in essentially the same strategic plight as the affluent but vastly outnumbered white population of South Africa today.

Even the United States, separated from the fast-growing population centres of Asia and Africa by two mighty oceans, is not immune. As Ivan Head observes, "North America is home to one of the fastest growing of all national populations. The population of Mexico in 1950 was 25 million. Before this decade concludes, it will be 100 million." Despite the magnetic power of US popular culture (which once made even the French feel threatened), some of the southwestern states of the United States are effectively becoming bilingual societies, reflecting the great influx from the south. At what point will the nature of US society and culture change irreversibly?

The term "population explosion" is disarmingly familiar, a cliché. But like many clichés it expresses a vital truth. From 1750 to 1950, the populations of the five main continents grew at about the same rate. After 1950, there was a dramatic surge of population growth in the Third World, largely resulting from the spread of Western methods of hygiene and basic health care. The population balance between Europe and North America and the rest of the world has been irretrievably altered. In the year 2000 (a mere eight years away), out of a projected global population of 6.25 billion, 5 billion will live in the Third World. Ninety-seven percent of the world's population increase will take place in the Third World.

Population numbers matter. When there are extreme differences, they create the sort of security dilemmas that, in their different ways, nations such as Israel, Mongolia, Nepal and white South Africa face. Even in the absence of such conventional security threats, this population imbalance, aggravated by the enormous disparity in living standards, will be the fundamental underlying cause of the new sorts of threats facing the Western world, ranging from migrations of the poor and dispossessed to environmental damage, drugs, disease and terrorism.

THE IMPACT OF EAST ASIA

The stark picture of an affluent West and a poor Third World is complicated and confused by the increasing importance of the East Asians, the only non-Westerners already in, or poised to enter, the world of developed nations. Though their economic success, especially that of Japan, is seen as a serious problem by some in the West, in the larger context of relations between the West and the Rest it should surely be seen as part of the solution. For Japan and the other East Asian success stories are setting off ripples of development in the Third World in a way that no Western society has ever succeeded in doing.

Consider this great historical oddity: Why is it that decades of proximity to, and contact with, North America and Western Europe did not inspire any of the neighbouring societies in Latin America, the Middle East or Africa to plunge into the free-market universe, despite the obvious economic benefits of doing so? Why is Japan the only developed nation to stimulate such emulation?

The answer will inevitably be complex, but one critical factor, largely overlooked, has been the psychological. In 1905, when Japan, an Asian nation, defeated Russia, a white power, it unintentionally provided a tremendous psychological boost to anti-colonialism. If not the vast majority, then at least the emerging educated elites of non-European countries could, for the first time, conceive of the possibility that colonial subjugation was not necessarily a permanent condition, a state of nature. The generation of Jawaharlal Nehru, a boy of 14 at the time of the war, was greatly stirred.

Today, Japan's economic success is having a similar psychological impact on developing societies all over the world, gradually convincing them that they too can make it into the developed universe. This psychological leap is crucial. Until recently, most Third World nations believed subconsciously that developed status was out of their reach. Today, after looking at Japan and its neighbours, many believe otherwise.

Japan did not intend this. Global benevolence has not yet infused the character of the Japanese. But its success convinced its neighbours, ranging from Korea to Taiwan to Singapore, that they too could do it. Their success has, in turn, had a significant effect on China. The economic take-off of China's coastal provinces has reduced the ability of Beijing to reverse course from economic liberalisation and has also helped convince Indonesia, the world's fifth most populous nation, to deregulate even faster, suggesting that a new economic synergy is developing in East Asia.

But the effect is not restricted to the region. Largely unnoticed, pilgrims from all other parts of the world have been coming to East Asia to observe and learn. Turks and Mexicans, Iranians and Chileans are fascinated by East Asia's success. If the East Asians can do it, why not they? So far no Islamic nation has successfully modernised. But if Malaysia and Indonesia, two Muslim countries far from the birthplace of Islam, can be swept along by the rising Asia-Pacific economic tide—and the process is well under way—the winds in the Islamic world will no longer move from West to East Asia but in the reverse direction, a major historic change. Over time, countries like Algeria and Tunisia may also be drawn into this process.

Looked at in this way, Europe and North America, which are increasingly feeling threatened by Japan's economic advance, may indeed have a vested interest in its progress. If the belief and expectation of economic development can be planted in the minds of billions of people, massive migrations may be averted. Those Western Europeans who are already fearful of such migrations from North Africa should do some fundamental strategic rethinking and begin viewing the challenge from East Asia in a different light. What is a short-term challenge could bring long-term strategic redemption.

ECONOMIC HORSES, DEMOCRATIC CARTS

As the numbers mount and the prospect of ever-worsening poverty and massive immigration looms, most of those Westerners who have not become entirely indifferent to the Third World seem to be determined that first priority must be given to the promotion of human rights and democracy. For the first time since decolonisation, many countries have been told that development aid, even from multilateral institutions like the UN Development Program, will be conditioned upon moves towards democratisation. This campaign for democracy and human rights in the Third World could backfire badly and undermine Western security in the post-Cold War era.

The collapse of communism in the face of challenges from democracies has given a powerful new burst of confidence in democratic values. These values strengthen the social and political fabric of Western societies because they involve all citizens in national affairs and hence develop in the citizens a commitment to their society. In addition, democratic systems lead to constant circulation within the ruling elites, thereby ensuring the infusion of new blood and new ideas into critical councils. As well as the moral strength of these values, their functional strengths will enhance the global trend towards democratisation and increasing respect for human rights. Those that fail to adapt to this trend are likely to suffer in the long-term Darwinian contest between societies. Japan, for example, could remain far ahead of China for centuries if China fails to create a system that will enable it to extract and use its human talent as effectively as Japan.

The question remains, however: How does one successfully transplant democracies into societies that historically have had very different social and political systems? The conventional wisdom in some American political and intellectual circles today is that any society, including China, can make this transition virtually immediately. Yet most Western societies (including the most recent cases, like Spain and Portugal) did not make the leap overnight from traditional or semi-feudal systems. Economic development came first, creating both working and middle classes that had a vested interest in stability and would therefore not be pulled apart by demagogic democratic politicians trying to capitalise on ethnic and other sectional differences. That has also been the path taken by those who have made the successful transition to democracy in East Asia.

Today, the West is encouraging, and sometimes demanding, the opposite approach in the Third World. It is promoting democracy *before* economic development. It assumes that democracy can be successfully transplanted into societies that are at low levels of economic development, and that are deeply divided socially across many lines—tribal, ethnic and religious, among others. In a developed and industrialised society, a democratic system draws in the established middle class that has a vested interest in stability. In many Asian and African cases, without such middle classes the national polity breaks down into ethnic and tribal loyalties. If this in turn leads to internecine warfare, can one argue that democracy will always bring beneficial consequences?

As far back as 1861, John Stuart Mill said that democracy is "next to impossible in a country made up of different nationalities." Even earlier, John Jay, writing in the *Federalist*, stressed that Americans were "descended from the same ancestors, speaking the same language, professing the same religion, attached to the same principles of government, very similar in their manners and customs." He added that they were surely "a band of brethren" and "should never be split into a number of unsocial, jealous and alien sovereignties." Earlier theorists of democracy would be surprised by the 20th-century conceit that democracy can be applied to any society, regardless of its stage of development or its internal social divisions.

To avoid misunderstanding, let me stress that I am not arguing that democratic systems are necessarily antithetical to development in contemporary Third World societies. Theoretically, it is possible to have both. In some cases, it may even work. But a calm and dispassionate look at Third World conditions suggests that a period of strong and firm government, one that is committed to radical reform, may be necessary to break out of the vicious circle of poverty sustained by social structures that contain vested interests opposed to any real changes. Japan was able to go into high growth after World War II in part because of the wide-ranging socio-economic reforms that General MacArthur imposed. No democratically elected Japanese government could have done what he did. By contrast, the failure of the United States to carry out similar socio-economic reforms in the Philippines is one reason why the economy of that country has not developed well in the postwar years.

Of course, the Filipino case demonstrates that authoritarian governments can be antithetical to development. However, it is equally true that some authoritarian governments have been good for development, as is shown by the dramatic economic growth of South Korea and Taiwan in the early years. The point here is simple: The crucial variable in determining whether a Third World society will progress is not whether its government is democratic but whether, to put it simply, it has "good government".

"Good government" is hard to define, especially in the American context, where the term is almost an oxymoron. In the United States, good government often means the least government. In Third World societies, burdened with huge development demands, the common characteristics found in the successful East Asian societies may help to provide a useful definition of "good government". These would include: (1) political stability, (2) sound bureaucracies based on meritocracy, (3) economic growth with equity, (4) fiscal prudence and (5) relative lack of corruption. With these criteria in mind, it should be possible for multilateral institutions like the World Bank to work out an operational definition that would determine eligibility for foreign aid.

The effect of such a reorientation of Western policies towards the Third World would be that less attention would be paid to the process by which Third World governments come into being and more attention would be paid to their performance. If their performance leads to serious and consistent improvement in the living conditions of the population, both the humanitarian and pragmatic considerations that underlie Western policies would be satisfied: the humanitarian because there would be less starvation and suffering, and the pragmatic because improving conditions would mean less migration to the West.

While human rights campaigns are often portrayed as an absolute moral good to be implemented without any qualifications, in practice Western governments are prudent and selective. For example, given their powerful vested interest in secure and stable oil supplies from Saudi Arabia, Western governments have not tried to export their standards of human rights or democracy to that country, for they know that any alternative to the stable rule of the Saudi government would very likely be bad for the West.

The recent Algerian experience introduces another complication for Western advocates of immediate democratisation. Democracies work all too well in bringing out the true social and cultural face of a society. In Algeria the centuries-old Islamic heritage had been suppressed by the secular and modern values introduced by the post-colonial elite. That Islamic heritage is now surfacing, and it will probably surface in other Islamic societies that hold democratic elections. If these governments elected by popular mandate impose strict Islamic laws that restrict some human rights (as Iran has), should we respect their right to decide their own values and practices? There are no easy answers.

The reaction of the West to the military coup in Algeria illustrates the moral and political ambiguities. Nominally, most Western governments have condemned the coup. However, in reaction to the questions posed by the citizens of France, Italy and Spain as to whether democracy in Algeria is good for their own countries, most Western governments have quietly welcomed the coup, a sensible pragmatic decision based on Western interests. In the eyes of many Third World observers this pragmatic application of moral values leads to a cynical belief that the West will only advance democracy when it suits its own interests. The same cynicism can develop—is almost certain to develop—over human rights campaigns. Would the West be as tough on the Chinese regime in Beijing if China were located where either Turkey or Mexico is today? Would the West then be as sanguine about the prospect of millions of boat people emerging from China if the regime broke down and chaos prevailed?

Take the case of Peru. In Peru, as in Algeria, there was a spectacular reversal in the trend towards democratisation. However, Peru was punished with sanctions, while Algeria was not. The Europeans wisely calculated that sanctions on Algeria would further destabilise the volatile socio-economic situation and exacerbate the flow of Algerian refugees. Hence, nothing was done. Peru was further away from any Western society. So even though sanctions would be equally destabilising in an equally volatile socio-economic environment, they were imposed.

Westerners should surely have asked: What kind of authoritarian government was Fujimori imposing? Was he going to become a Marcos and enrich his personal coffers, or was he desperately trying to reverse course for a society on the verge of serious breakdown? Do such questions matter? Curiously, few have noticed that if *current* Western policies had been in force in the 1950s and 1960s, the spectacular economic growth of Taiwan and South Korea could have been cut off at its very inception by the demand that the governments then in place be dismantled.

In Peru, one additional cause for concern is that if the sanctions succeed in their purpose of unseating the Fujimori government, the possible alternatives of chaos or a Latin American version of Pol Potism could be much worse for the Peruvian people. Those who firmly advocate sanctions on Peru should be prepared to accept moral responsibility for the consequences of those sanctions, good or bad. If they do so, the world may avoid a repetition of the Cambodian experience, where all those who advocated the removal of the Lon Nol regime refused to accept moral responsibility for the genocide that followed. If the West chooses to be prudent in targeting human rights abuses where its own interests are involved, does it not have an obligation to exercise the same prudence when others may be affected by these campaigns?

In the face of these moral and political complexities, Western governments may find it in their interest to explain to their citizens that prudence may have to be a crucial consideration in the promotion of human rights and democracy. Unfortunately, while Western governments are prudent in practice, they find it almost impossible to speak honestly to their own citizens on the subject. Philosophically, it is difficult to discuss prudence in promoting democratisation; it is not an uplifting, inspirational virtue. Yet both honesty and self-interest suggest that Western governments should do so.

No Western government has publicly confessed that in determining its particular human rights and democracy policies, it weighs them against other vital national interests. Yet every government does so: The Germans take a strong stand on Kurdish rights, the United States does not. The United States and the United Kingdom come down hard on Qaddafi, Italy does not. This pattern of inconsistencies in turn undervalues the merit of these human rights policies in the eyes of the ostensible beneficiaries, the Third World societies, because instead of being impressed by the moral courage of Western governments, they notice the pragmatic and calculated application of moral principles.

The human rights campaigns launched by Western governments and non-governmental organisations have done much good. They have, for example, created a new global consensus that militates against the return of gross and egregious violators of human rights like Pol Pot, Idi Amin and Boukassa. The victims of such regimes can breathe a sigh of relief. Similarly, the strong global consensus against the gross forms of torture that prevailed in many parts of the world is a great advance in human history.

But from the viewpoint of many Third World citizens, human rights campaigns often have a bizarre quality. For many of them it looks something like this: They are like hungry and diseased passengers on a leaky, overcrowded boat that is about to drift into treacherous waters, in which many of them will perish. The captain of the boat is often harsh, sometimes fairly and sometimes not. On the river banks stand a group of affluent, well-fed and well-intentioned onlookers. As soon as those onlookers witness a passenger being flogged or imprisoned or even deprived of his right to speak, they board the ship to intervene, protecting the passengers from the captain. But those passengers remain hungry and diseased. As soon as they try to swim to the banks into the arms of their benefactors, they are firmly returned to the boat, their primary sufferings unabated. This is no abstract analogy. It is exactly how the Haitians feel.

In the long run, it may be wiser for the West to encourage a more viable process of transition in developing societies, one that puts the horse before the cart—promoting economic development through good government before promoting democracy. This is not to argue that the international community should tolerate vicious dictators like Pol Pot or Idi Amin as long as they promote economic development. Rather, Third World governments should be treated with the same degree of pragmatic realism as is already applied to the governments of Algeria, Morocco and Tunisia by European governments.

Implementing this apparently simple reversal would be very difficult for most Western governments. Promoting democracy in most cases involves little in the way of costs or sacrifices. But promoting economic development has significant costs, direct or indirect. What may be good for the Third World in the long run (promoting economic development first) could prove painful for Western societies in the short run. The EC would, for example, need to abandon its massive subsidies to inefficient European farmers. If the West persists in taking the easy road in the short run, promoting democracy first, it will ultimately prove painful and costly because the effects of massive Third World poverty and instability will appear on its doorstep. Unfortunately, when there is a conflict between the short-term and the long-term in democratic politics, it is usually safer to bet that short-term considerations will prevail.

WESTERN DEMOCRACY VS. WESTERN INTERESTS

The record of Western democracies in overcoming the various challenges they have faced is impressive. Unlike Athens, they have so far triumphed in both peace and war. The resilience of these societies should never be underestimated. Yet it is dangerous to assume that they have no institutional defects.

In the absence of a clear and imminent threat, most Western governments find it difficult to convince their populations that given the seriousness of the post-Cold War challenges, they must be prepared to accept some painful changes and sacrifices. The problem is not lack of leadership in these societies, but institutional arrangements.

The global effects of these institutional defects of democracy can be demonstrated with two examples, both of which have harmed the non-Western world a great deal: the US budget deficit and the EC Common Agricultural Policy (CAP).

Despite a wide consensus in the United States that budget deficits have to be stopped, the budget has effectively become a monster that no government institution can effectively tame. Gramm-Rudman failed miserably. The problem arises out of institutional defects in the democratic system. The interlocking network of votes by the various lobbies means that they have a stranglehold on the budget process, thereby guaranteeing the perpetuation of the enormous deficits.

Private lobbies distort the economic competitiveness of the United States in other ways, with ramifications that spill outside US borders. For example, as far back as the early 1980s, the US auto industry asked for and, through the intervention of the US government, received respite from Japanese competition in the form of voluntary restraints. In the decade that followed, the industry, instead of trying to learn from Japan and investing in competitiveness, continued to pay both its shareholders and management rich dividends. No effort was made to check whether this public intervention was being used for public or private good. The Japanese government's intervention in the Japanese economy is done with the clear understanding that long-term Japanese national interests lie in enhancing, not undermining, the international competitiveness of Japanese industries. Not so in the United States, where government institutions respond to ad hoc pressures from private interests.

The CAP is another monster that has been created out of the institutional defects of Western democracies. In private, virtually no EC leader can defend the CAP. In public, no French or Spanish or Italian leader would criticise it for fear of not being elected.

By absorbing over two-thirds of the EC budget, the CAP draws funding away from industries that could enhance the EC's competitiveness. It has also crippled the GATT discussions because the non-EC nations see no reason why they should accept painful changes when the affluent EC nations will not do so. Why, for example, should Indonesia, Brazil and Zaire—three nations that could form an "oxygen cartel"—curb their lucrative deforestation activities when the affluent EC societies will not accept any sacrifices? Only the lack of awareness of such problems can explain why the crippling of the Uruguay Round of GATT talks in December 1990 was allowed to happen by the West. This crippling seriously aggravated the new threats that the West faces in the post-Cold War era.

To prevent massive migrations from the poor to the affluent societies, a significant burst of economic development would be needed around the globe. One crucial global instrument that is needed to trigger such widespread economic development is GATT. If all societies abide by its rules, it creates a single and massive global marketplace that all societies, rich and poor, can plug into. GATT has already demonstrated its power by carrying a significant portion of mankind— those living in the West—to the highest levels of comfort and affluence enjoyed in the history of man. It does this quite simply by creating a "level playing field" in which each society can exploit its comparative economic advantage. The impact on global productivity has been enormous.

There were few protests when the Uruguay Round was crippled in December 1990. Perhaps it was seen as merely a "trade" issue. The Brussels meeting failed because the European Community wanted to protect certain industries from global competition. This will eventually prove futile because capitalism is fundamentally a dynamic process. In trying to protect their industries from new competition, the West is trying to freeze an unfreezable process.

Given the historical impact it has already had and its relevance to the central problems of the immediate future, it is puzzling that more strategic thinkers have not focused on the GATT. It is a mistake not to do so. By denying the vast masses an opportunity to improve their livelihood, a retreat from the GATT to protectionism will force them to pound on the doors of the West.

Reorienting Western strategy in the post-Cold War era is a major task, requiring the sort of leadership that the United States so handsomely provided after World War II. Unfortunately, at the end of the Cold War, the leadership of the West has fractured between the United States, Europe and Japan at the very moment when the need for leadership in the Western world has never been greater. Unfortunately, too, Western societies are under strong pressure to turn inwards when they should be looking outwards. Having created a technology that has brought the world, with all of its attendant problems and promises, to its very doorstep, the West now has a strong impulse to shut the doors, a futile impulse. Futile because it has created a universe in which "interconnectedness" will be the order of the day.

The real danger is that the West will realise too late that—like the defenders of Singapore—it has been preoccupied with old challenges while new ones have been assuming massive proportions.

AN ASIAN PERSPECTIVE ON HUMAN RIGHTS AND FREEDOM OF THE PRESS

TEXT OF LECTURE AT SEMINAR ON "ASIAN AND AMERICAN PERSPECTIVES ON CAPITALISM AND DEMOCRACY" IN SINGAPORE. 28–30 JANUARY 1993.

In January 1993 the Asia Society of New York and three Singapore institutions—the Institute of Southeast Asian Studies, the Singapore International Foundation and the Institute of Policy Studies—organised a seminar on "Asian and American Perspectives on Capitalism and Democracy" in Singapore. I was asked to give the Asian perspective on human rights and freedom of the press. James Fallows, my fellow panellist, was shocked and disturbed by my paper. I spelled out 10 heresies, which I believed the West had either ignored or suppressed, and added five principles that could lead to a dialogue of equals between Asia and America. Since I touched on so many sacred cows, I assumed that Western journals, which loved controversy, would want to publish it. However, none were interested until the *Washington Quarterly* bravely published a shorter version entitled "Go East, Young Man". The longer version that follows is also being published in a collection of essays entitled *Debating Human Rights*, edited by Peter Van Ness.

I would like to begin with an analogy, but I apologise to those who may have heard me recount it before:

> … from the viewpoint of many Third World citizens, human rights campaigns often have a bizarre quality. For many of them it looks something like this: They are like hungry and diseased passengers on a leaky, overcrowded boat that is about to drift into treacherous waters, in which many of them will perish. The captain of the boat is often harsh, sometimes fairly and sometimes not. On the river banks stand a group of affluent, well-fed, and well-intentioned onlookers. As soon as those onlookers witness a passenger being flogged or imprisoned or even deprived of his right to speak, they board the ship to intervene, protecting the passengers from the captain. But those passengers remain hungry and diseased. As soon as they try to swim to the banks into the arms of their benefactors, they are firmly returned to the boat, their primary sufferings unabated. This is no abstract analogy. It is exactly how the Haitians feel.[1]

This is just one of the many absurd aspects of the aggressive Western promotion of human rights at the end of the Cold War. There are many others. Yet, when I tried in seminars at Harvard University to challenge the universal applicability of democracy, human rights or freedom of the press, I discovered that these values have become virtual "sacred cows". No one could challenge their intrinsic worth. Worse still, when I persisted, I was greeted with sniggers, smug looks and general derision. The general assumption there was that any Asian, especially a Singaporean, who challenged these concepts was doing so only in an attempt to cover up the sins of his government.

I am as convinced now as I was then that the aggressive Western promotion of democracy, human rights and freedom of the press to the Third World at the end of the Cold War was, and is, a colossal mistake. This campaign is unlikely to benefit the 4.3 billion people who live outside the developed world, and perhaps not even the 700 million people who live inside it. This campaign could aggravate, rather than ameliorate, the difficult conditions under which the vast majority of the world's population live.

But to get this central point into Western minds, one must first remove the barriers that have made these topics into untouchable sacred cows in Western discourse. A Westerner must first acknowledge that when he discusses these topics with a non-Westerner, he is, consciously or unconsciously, standing behind a pulpit. If it is any consolation, let me hasten to add that this attitude is not new. As the following passage from the *Dictionary of the History of Ideas* indicates, it goes back centuries:

> The concept of despotism began as a distinctively European perception of Asian governments and practices: Europeans as such were considered to be free by nature, in contrast to the servile nature of the Orientals. Concepts of despotism have frequently been linked to justifications, explanations, or arraignments of slavery, conquest, and colonial or imperial domination. The attribution of despotism to an enemy may be employed to mobilize the members of a political unit, or those of a regional area. Thus the Greeks stigmatized the Persians as despotic in much the same way that Christian writers were to treat the Turks. By an irony not always perceived either by the purported champions of liberty against despotism, or by their historians, such arguments often became the rationale, as in Aristotle, for the domination by those with a tradition of liberty over others who had never enjoyed that happy condition.[2]

On the eve of the 21st century this European attitude to Asians has to come to an end. The assumption of moral superiority must be abandoned. A level playing field needs to be created for meaningful discussions between Asians and Americans. That will be my first goal in this paper. In the second half, I will put across the view of one Asian on human rights and freedom of the press.

A LEVEL PLAYING FIELD

It is never a pleasant experience to be lowered from a pedestal. I apologise for any psychological discomfort that my remarks may cause. Yet, to achieve this objective in one paper, I will have to be ruthless if I am to be brief. To remove the "sacred cow" dimension surrounding the subjects of human rights and freedom of the press, I propose to list 10 heresies that the West, including the United States, has either ignored, suppressed or pretended to be irrelevant or inconsequential in its discussions on these subjects. If these heresies have any validity at all, I hope that this will lead Western writers to accept that they do not have a monopoly of wisdom or virtue on these subjects and that they should try to exercise a little more humility when they discourse on these subjects to a non-Western audience.

Heresy No. 1: American journalists do not believe in the Christian rule "Do unto others as you would have others do unto you".
From Gary Hart to Bill Clinton, there has developed an honourable journalistic tradition that the infidelities of a politician are public property, to be exposed in every detail. But those who participate in this tradition do not feel themselves bound by Jesus Christ's statement "Let he who has not sinned cast the first stone".

To the best of my limited knowledge, based on my short stay in Washington, DC, the level of infidelities seemed about the same in all sectors of society, whether in Congress or in the press corps. Power proves to be a great aphrodisiac. Both politicians and journalists have equal difficulty resisting the temptations that flow their way. Yet, the actions of one group are deemed immoral and subject to public scrutiny, while those of the other are deemed private matters. But in the informal pecking order worked out in Washington, DC (as in any other tribal society) many a senior journalist enjoys far more effective power than a congressman. But they are subject to different levels of scrutiny.

The same disparity applies to personal finances. All aspiring politicians, even the few unfortunate ones who may have entered politics to do a service to the nation, have to declare every penny of their financial worth. Yet none of the Washington, DC journalists, many of whom enjoy far greater incomes, feel any moral obligation to declare all their financial worth; nor do they feel any need to declare how their own financial worth would be enhanced by discussing the financial worth of an aspiring politician. A full disclosure of income and wealth on the part of those who make, and those who influence, public policy decisions (including lobbyists and journalists) will probably indicate the great mismatch in financial muscle between the actual policymakers and those who seek to influence them. It may also help to illuminate why, despite so many rational discussions, so many irrational public policy choices are made.

Heresy No. 2: Power corrupts. The absolute power of the Western journalist in the Third World corrupts absolutely.

The greatest myth that a journalist cherishes is that he is an underdog: the lone ranger who works against monstrous bureaucracies to uncover the real truth, often at great personal risk. I never understood this myth when I was in Washington, DC. Cabinet secretaries, senators and congressmen, ambassadors and generals promptly returned the phone calls of, and assiduously cultivated, the journalists in Washington, DC. Not all these powerful office-holders were as good as Kissinger or Jim Baker in seducing American journalists, but none would dare tell an American journalist of a major paper to go to hell. It was as inconceivable as trying to exercise dissent in the court of Attila the Hun.

The cruellest results of this myth are experienced in the developing world. On arriving in a Third World capital, no American journalist would shake out from his unconsciousness the deeply embedded myth that he was once again arriving as a lone ranger battling an evil and corrupt Third World government. Never would he admit that he had arrived in a Third World capital with as much power as a colonial proconsul in the 19th century. In both cases the host government ignored these emissaries at its own peril. The average correspondent from an influential Western journal who arrived in a Third World capital would, of course, ask to see the president, prime minister and perhaps foreign minister. If, heaven forbid, any of these leaders should refuse, this would be a typical response: "Given that Kings and Presidents throughout the world regularly grant interviews to *The Guardian* (please note our recent exclusive interview with the King of Jordan) and, indeed, sometimes write in *The Guardian* (as with former President Gorbachev), I do wonder by what token *The Guardian* is not considered worthy of such a request. We are, after all, the second highest selling quality national daily in the UK." (Note: this is an extract from an actual letter.)

A Western journalist would be thoroughly puzzled by a request for reciprocity from, say, a journalist from the *Times of India* in Washington, DC. Pressed for a justification for this imbalance, he would dismiss the case for reciprocity on the grounds that the *New York Times* (NYT), for example, is a better paper than the *Times of India*. Never would he admit to himself that the prime minister, even of India, would hesitate to turn down an NYT request knowing that the NYT controlled the gateways to key minds in Washington, DC. What is sweet about this exercise of power by an NYT correspondent is that he would never have to admit that he was savouring the delicious fruits of power, since they come with no obvious trappings of office.

Heresy No. 3: A free press can serve as the opium of society.
This statement is not quite as outrageous as Marx's dictum that religion can serve as the opium of the people, but it will probably be dismissed as quickly as Marx's statement was when he first uttered it. The American media prides itself on the ability of its investigative journalism to uncover the real truth behind the stories put out by government, big business and other major institutions. It could never stomach the proposition that it could serve as the opium of American society. But it has.

In the last 20 years there have been two parallel developments. First, American journalism has become much more aggressive than it ever was. Kennedy was the last US president to be treated with kid gloves; his sexual excesses were well known but not publicised. Since then no US president has been considered off-limits for total coverage, giving the impression that the US government is under total and close scrutiny.

The parallel trend is this. The last 20 years have also seen increasingly bad government. Lyndon Johnson felt that he could fight a war and create a good society without raising taxes. This began the process of fiscal indiscipline. Richard Nixon's flaws are well known, as are Jimmy Carter's. In the last 12 years, under two Republican administrations, the United States has gone from being the world's largest creditor country to being the world's largest debtor country. A Swiss investment consultant, Jean Antoine Cramer, noted recently, "It took 150 years for the US government to create a debt of $1000bn, and only 10 years to quadruple this debt. With a GNP of $5600bn, the situation is beyond repair. American consumers owe $7000bn, corporations $5000bn and the government $5000bn." No American politician, in the land of the free press, dares to utter any hard truths on the sacrifices needed to stop this rot. The consequence has been irresponsible government on a mind-boggling and historically unparalleled scale. Equally striking are the parallel troubles of some of the largest US corporations, including previous blue-chip names, such as Citicorp, GM and IBM, all of whom have also been under close scrutiny by the press.

It would be impossible for me, even if I had the whole day, to prove that there is a causal connection between a more aggressive free press and increasingly bad government. It may have been purely a coincidence. After all, the US press has been second to none in exposing the follies of the US government. But have all their exposures served as opiates, creating the illusion that something is being done when really nothing is being done?

There may be an even more cruel example of the free press serving as an opiate. One of the post-World War II achievements that the United States is very proud of is the political emancipation of African-Americans. The press played a key role in this. But did this emancipation in turn foster the illusion that the fundamental problems of the African-Americans had been solved? The impression given was that equality had finally been given to the African-Americans. The doors had been opened. All they had to do was to walk through.

Thirty years after the famous Civil Rights marches, if one were to ask an average African-American family, "Are you better off than you were 30 years ago?" how many would say yes and how many would say no? What did the large-scale rioting after the Rodney King episode demonstrate? That perhaps 30 years of discussion of African-Americans' problems have served as a substitute for 30 years of action, creating an illusion of movement when there has been little or none. Is it enough for the US media to say, "We did the best we can"? Or should it begin to ask, "Did we contribute to this failure in any way?"

Can the minds generated by the freest press in the world conceive of such questions?

Heresy No. 4: A free press need not lead to a well-ordered society.
A key assumption in the West is that a good society needs a free press to keep abuse of power in check. That freedom of information checks bad government. That its absence leads to greater abuses and bad government.

This may well be true. A free press can lead to good government. But this is not necessarily a true proposition. A free press can also lead to bad government.

In Southeast Asia we have seen an unfortunate demonstration of this. By far, the one country in Southeast Asia that has enjoyed the freest press for the longest period of time (except for the Marcos martial law interregnum) is the Philippines. But the Philippines is also the ASEAN society that is having the greatest difficulty in modernisation and economic progress, suggesting that a free press is neither a necessary nor a sufficient condition for development and progress.

India and China provide two massive social laboratories to judge what prescriptions would help a society develop and prosper. Between them, they hold about two-fifths of the world's population—two out of every five human beings on the planet. Each has taken a very different political road. The West approves the freedom of the press in India, frowns on the lack of it in China. Yet which society is developing faster today, and which society is likely to modernise first?

The recent Ayodhya incident demonstrated one important new dimension for societies all around the globe. The Indian media tried to control emotional reactions by restricting the broadcasting and distribution of video scenes of the destruction of the mosque. But now many Indian homes can see video clips (transmitted through satellites and tapes) from foreign news agencies, which felt no reason to exercise social, political or moral restraint. Those who happily transmitted the video clips never had to bear the consequences themselves. They were sitting comfortably in Atlanta, Georgia, or Hong Kong, while the riots that followed in India as a result of their TV transmissions never reached their homes. Unfortunately, these media personnel did not stop to consider whether they could have saved other human lives, not their own, by exercising restraint.

Heresy No. 5: Western journalists, in covering non-Western events, are conditioned by both Western prejudices and Western interests. The claim of "objective" reporting is a major falsehood.
Let me cite three major examples. First, the coverage of Islam. Edward W. Said, in his book *Covering Islam*, states:

> The hardest thing to get most academic experts on Islam to admit is that what they say and do as scholars is set in a profoundly and in some ways an offensively political context. Everything about the study of Islam in the contemporary West is saturated with political importance, but hardly any

writers on Islam, whether expert or general, admit the fact in what they say. Objectivity is assumed to inhere in learned discourse about other societies, despite the long history of political, moral, and religious concern felt in all societies, Western or Islamic, about the alien, the strange and different. In Europe, for example, the Orientalist has traditionally been affiliated directly with colonial offices: what we have just begun to learn about the extent of close cooperation between scholarship and direct military colonial conquest (as in the case of revered Dutch Orientalist C. Snouck Hurgronje, who used the confidence he had won from Muslims to plan and execute the brutal Dutch war against the Atjehnese people of Sumatra) is both edifying and depressing. Yet books and articles continue to pour forth extolling the nonpolitical nature of Western scholarship, the fruits of Orientalist learning, and the value of "objective" expertise. At the very same time there is scarcely an expert on "Islam" who has not been a consultant or even an employee of the government, the various corporations, the media. My point is that the cooperation must be admitted and taken into account, not just for moral reasons, but for intellectual reasons as well.[3]

Second, the US media coverage of the Vietnam War, a major event, some say a glorious chapter, in the history of US journalism. By the late 1960s and early 1970s, as American bodies were brought back from Vietnam, American public sentiment turned against the war. The United States had to get out. The US media helped to manufacture a justification: that the United States was supporting the "bad guys" (the crooked and wicked Saigon and Phnom Penh regimes) against the "good guys" (the dedicated incorruptible revolutionaries in North Vietnam or the Cambodian jungles). Books like *Fire in the Lake*, a glorification of the Vietnamese revolution, became the bible of American reporters. When the last American soldier left Vietnam, most American journalists felt satisfied and vindicated.

The subsequent communist victories in Cambodia and Vietnam exposed the true nature of the revolutionaries. The story of the Cambodian genocide is well known, as is the story of the thousands of boat people who perished in the South China Sea. The level of human misery increased, not decreased, after the revolution. Yet virtually no American journalist came forth to admit that perhaps he had been wrong in quoting from *Fire in the Lake* or in calling for the abandonment of the Saigon and Phnom Penh regimes. As long as American journalists had fulfilled vital US interests by saving American lives, they did not feel there was any need for them to weigh the moral consequences of their actions on non-Americans—the Vietnamese or the Cambodians.

Third, the coverage of the Tiananmen Square incident, a Chinese event that became a global media event. The essential Western media story is that it was a revolution by Chinese democrats against Chinese autocrats. The constant portrayal of the replica of the Statue of Liberty provided the pictorial image for this. Yet for all its massive coverage of Tiananmen, the Western media failed to explain how this event was seen through Chinese eyes. Few Chinese intellectuals believe that China is ready for democracy. Most are as afraid of chaos and anarchy (a persistent Chinese disease) as they are of a return to Maoist totalitarianism. It was a battle between soft authoritarians and hard authoritarians. The Western media vividly reported the apparent victory of the "hardliners", but it has failed to tell the world the true aftermath: the soft authoritarians have come back to power.

During Tiananmen, several Western journalists were blatantly dishonest. They would lunch with a student on a "hunger strike" before reporting on his "hunger". They were not all bystanders reporting on an event; several advised the students how to behave. None stayed to deal with the consequences that the students had to face.

The biggest indication of how American journalists are affected by US interests in their portrayal of China is to compare their reporting of China in the early 1970s and the early 1990s. When Nixon landed in China in 1972, the US media had a virtual love-fest with a regime that had just killed millions in the cultural revolution. Yet, in the 1990s a much more benign regime that has liberated millions from poverty and indignity and promises to launch them on the road to development is treated as a pariah regime.

Heresy No. 6: Western governments work with genocidal rulers when it serves their interests to do so.
It was August 1942, a dark moment in World War II. Churchill had flown secretly to Moscow to bring some bad news personally to Stalin: the Allies were not ready for a second front in Europe. Stalin reacted angrily. Nancy Caldwell Sorel, who describes that meeting, writes:

> Discord continued, but on the last evening, when Churchill went to say goodbye, Stalin softened … the hour that Churchill had planned for extended to seven. Talk and wine flowed freely, and in a moment of rare intimacy, Stalin admitted that even the stresses of war did not compare to the terrible struggle to force the collective farm policy on the peasantry. Millions of Kulaks had been, well, eliminated. The historian Churchill thought of Burke's dictum "If I cannot have reform without justice, I will not have reform," but the politician Churchill concluded that with the war requiring unity, it was best not to moralize aloud.[4]

The story elicits a chuckle. What a shrewd old devil Churchill was. How cunning of him not to displease Stalin with mere moralising. Neither then nor now has Churchill's reputation been sullied by his association with a genocidal ruler. Now change the cast of characters to an identical set: Margaret Thatcher and Pol Pot. Historically, they could have met, but of course they never did. Now try to describe a possible meeting and try to get a chuckle out of it. Impossible? Why?

Think about it. Think hard, for in doing so you will discover to your surprise that it is possible for thoughtful and well-informed people to have double standards. If the rule that prevents any possible meeting between Margaret Thatcher and Pol Pot is "thou shalt not have any discourse with a genocidal ruler," then the same rule also forbids any meeting between Stalin and Churchill. Moral rules, as the English philosopher R.M. Hare has stressed, are inherently universalisable. If we do want to allow a meeting between Churchill and Stalin (since, until the last few weeks, no historian has ever condemned Churchill, that must be the prevailing sentiment), then the rule has to be modified to "thou shalt not have any discourse with a genocidal ruler, unless there are mitigating circumstances."

This is not a mere change of nuance. We have made a fundamental leap, a leap best understood with an analogy contained in the following tale. A man meets a woman and asks her whether she would spend the night with him for a million dollars. She replies, "For a million dollars, sure."

He says, "How about five dollars?"

She replies indignantly, "What do you think I am?"

He replies, "We have already established what you are. We are only negotiating the price."

All those who condone Churchill's meeting with Stalin but would readily condemn any meeting with Pol Pot belong in the woman's shoes (logically speaking).

In Stalin's case, as England's survival was at stake, all was excused. In Pol Pot's case, as no conceivable vital Western interest could be served in any meeting with him, no mitigating excuse could possibly exist. Hence the total and absolute Western condemnation of any contact with Pol Pot or his minions in the Khmer Rouge. The tragedy for the Cambodian people is that the West, in applying this absolute moral rule only because its own vital interests were not involved, did not stop to ask whether the sufferings of the Cambodians could have been mitigated if the West had been as flexible in its dealings with the Khmer Rouge as Churchill had been with Stalin.

Throughout the 1980s, when several Asian governments were trying to achieve a viable Cambodian peace settlement (which would invariably have to include the Khmer Rouge), they were vilified for their direct contacts with the Khmer Rouge. American diplomats were instructed never to shake hands with Khmer Rouge representatives.

In the last 12 months, the atrocities committed by Radovan Karadzic and his Serbian followers (in full view of the US media) should be sufficient justification to put them in the same league as Pol Pot or Idi Amin. Yet, no Western diplomat has hesitated to shake the hands of these Serbian representatives. Is there one standard for Westerners and another for Asians?

Heresy No. 7: Western governments will happily sacrifice the human rights of Third World societies when it suits Western interests to do so.
The regime in Myanmar overturned the results of the democratic elections in 1990 and brutally suppressed the popular demonstrations that followed. Myanmar was punished with Western sanctions. Asian governments were criticised for not enthusiastically following suit.

The regime in Algeria overturned the results of the democratic elections in 1992 and brutally suppressed the popular demonstrations that followed. Algeria was not punished with Western sanctions. The Asian governments have never been provided with an explanation for this obvious double standard.

But the reasons are obvious. The fear of Western sanctions triggering off greater political instability, leading to thousands of boat people crossing the tiny Mediterranean Sea into Europe, made the EC governments prudent and cautious. Despite this, they had no hesitation in criticising Asian governments for exercising the same prudence for the same reasons when it came to applying sanctions against Myanmar or China. Double standards, by any moral criteria, are obviously immoral. How many Western papers have highlighted this?

Heresy No. 8: The West has used the pretext of human rights abuses to abandon Third World allies that no longer serve Western interests.
The "sins" of Mohd. Siad Barre (Somalia), Mobutu (Zaire) and Daniel Arap Moi (Kenya) were as well known during the Cold War as they

are now. They did not convert from virtue to vice the day the Cold War ended. Yet, behaviour that was deemed worthy of Western support during the Cold War was deemed unacceptable when the Cold War ended.

It is remarkable how much satisfaction the Western governments, media and public have taken over their ability finally to pursue "moral" policies after the end of the Cold War. Yet, this has not come with any admission that the West was (logically speaking) pursuing "immoral" policies during the Cold War. Nor has anyone addressed the question of whether it is "honourable" to use and abandon allies.

Heresy No. 9: The West cannot acknowledge that the pursuit of "moral" human rights policies can have immoral consequences.

At the end of the Paris International Conference on Cambodia (ICC) in August 1989, the then Vietnamese foreign minister, Nguyen Co Thach, insisted that the conference declaration should call for a non-return of the genocidal policies and practices of the Khmer Rouge. All present there knew that Nguyen Co Thach was not really that concerned about Pol Pot's record. (Indeed, Thach once made the mistake of privately confessing to congressman Stephen Solarz that Vietnam did not invade Cambodia to save the Cambodian people from Pol Pot, even though this was the official Vietnamese propaganda line.) However, Thach knew that the Khmer Rouge, a party to the Paris conference, would not accept such a reference. Hence, the conference would fail, a failure that the Vietnamese wanted because they were not ready then to relinquish control of Cambodia. Western officials did not dare to challenge him for fear that Nguyen Co Thach would expose them to their own media. At the same time, despite having scuttled a conference that could have brought peace to Cambodia, Nguyen Co Thach came out smelling good in the eyes of the Western media because he had taken a strong stand against the Khmer Rouge. Yet, in practical terms, from the viewpoint of the ordinary Cambodian, the strong Western consensus against the Khmer Rouge had backfired against the Cambodians because it prevented the Western delegations from exposing Nguyen Co Thach's blatant scuttling of the peace conference. Out of good (the Western media condemnation of Pol Pot) came evil (the destruction of a peace conference). This was not the first time it had happened in history. As Max Weber said in his famous essay "Politics As a Vocation", "... it is *not* true that good can only follow from good and evil only from evil, but that often the opposite is true. Anyone who says this is, indeed, a political infant."[5]

The morally courageous thing for a Western delegate to have done at that Paris conference would have been to stand up in front of the Western media and explain why the inclusion of the Khmer Rouge was necessary if one wanted a peace agreement to end the Cambodians' sufferings. No Western leader even dreamt of doing so, so strong was the sentiment against the Khmer Rouge. This produced a curious contradiction for moral philosophers: the ostensibly morally correct position (i.e., of excluding the Khmer Rouge) produced immoral consequences—prolonging the Cambodians' agony.

This was not by any means the first of such moral dilemmas confronted by Western officials. Max Weber asserts, "No ethics in the world can dodge the fact that in numerous instances the attainment of 'good' ends is bound to the fact that one must be willing to pay the price of using morally dubious means or at least dangerous ones ...."[6] Unfortunately, there is no living Western statesman who has the courage to make such a statement, for in the era of "political correctness" that we live in, the Western media would excoriate any such brave soul. Out of moral correctness, we have produced moral cowardice.

Heresy No. 10: An imperfect government that commits some human rights violations is better than no government, in many societies.
At least two nation-states have broken apart since the end of the Cold War—Somalia and Yugoslavia. Both shared a common characteristic of being useful to the West in the Cold War. The sins of their

governments were forgiven then. When these ruling regimes were abandoned (each in a different way), the net result was an increase in human misery. A utilitarian moral philosopher would have no difficulty arguing that the previous situation of imperfect government was a better moral choice because it caused less misery.

The inability of the West to accept this can lead to a repetition of Yugoslavia's and Somalia's experiences. Take Peru, for example. It was drifting towards chaos and anarchy. President Fujimori imposed emergency rule to halt the slide. He should have been praised for his courage in taking decisive action to prevent anarchy. However, because the form of his action, a temporary retreat from parliamentary rule, was deemed unacceptable by the West, the beneficial consequences of his action for the Peruvian people were ignored by the West. In trying to maintain its form of ideological purity, the West was prepared to sacrifice the interests of the Peruvian people.

If current Western policies of punishing authoritarian governments had been in force in the 1960s and 1970s, the spectacular economic growth of Taiwan and South Korea would have been cut off at its very inception by Western demands that the governments then in power be replaced by less authoritarian regimes. Instead, by allowing the authoritarian governments, which were fully committed to economic development, to run the full course, the West has brought about the very economic and social changes that have paved the way for the more open and participative societies that Taiwan and South Korea have become. The lessons from East Asia are clear. There are no short cuts. It is necessary for a developing society to first succeed in economic development before it can attain the social and political freedoms found in the developed societies.

There is no unified Asian view on human rights and freedom of the press. These are Western concepts. Asians are obliged to react to them. Predictably, there is a whole range of reactions, ranging from those who subscribe to these concepts in toto to those who reject them completely. An understanding of the Asian reactions is clouded by the fact that many Asians feel obliged to pay at least lip service to their values. For example, many Japanese intellectuals, who remain children of the Meiji Restoration in their belief that Japan should become more Western than Asian, proclaim their adherence to Western values on human rights, although they have a curious inability to discuss Japan's record in World War II in the same breath. From New Delhi to Manila, to name just two cities, there are many strong believers in these values. But in most Asian societies there is little awareness, let alone understanding, of these concepts. The truth is that the vast continent of Asia, preoccupied with more immediate challenges, has not had the time or energy to address these issues squarely.

I shall, therefore, make no pretence of speaking on behalf of Asia, although I am reasonably confident that my views will not be dismissed as eccentric by most Asians. My hope today is to find some credible middle ground where both Asians and Americans can have a dialogue as equals and with equally legitimate points of view. I will be so bold as to venture five principles that should guide such a discourse.

Principle No. 1: Mutual respect

The first principle that I want to stress is that all discussions between Asians and Americans on the subject of human rights and freedom of the press should be based on mutual respect. I have visited the offices of four great American newspapers: the *New York Times*, the *Washington Post*, the *Los Angeles Times* and the *Wall Street Journal*. In any one of the four offices, if you ventured out at night and strayed a few hundred yards off course, you would be putting your life in jeopardy. Yet, despite this, none of the editorial desks or writers would argue in favour of the reduction of the civil liberties of habitual criminals. Danger from habitual crime is considered an acceptable price to pay for no reduction in liberty. This is one social choice.

In Singapore, you can wander out at night in any direction from the *Straits Times* office and not put your life in jeopardy. One reason for this is that habitual criminals and drug addicts are locked up, often for long spells, until they have clearly reformed. The interest of the majority in having safe city streets is put ahead of considerations of rigorous due process, although safeguards are put in place to ensure that innocent individuals are not locked up. This is another kind of social choice. Let me suggest that none is intrinsically superior. Let those who make the choice live with the consequences of their choice. Similarly, if this statement can be received without the usual Western sniggers, let me add that a city that bans the sale of chewing gum has as much moral right to do so as a city that effectively allows the sale of crack on its streets. Let us try to avoid the knee-jerk smug response that one choice is more moral than the other.

I do not want to belabour this point, but it will be psychologically difficult for the West to accept the notion that alternative social and political choices can deserve equal respect. For 500 years, the West has been dominant in one form or another. After World War II most of Asia, like much of the Third World, was politically emancipated. But the process of mental emancipation, on the parts of both the colonised and the colonisers, is taking much longer. This explains why Chris Patten can march into Hong Kong, five years before its date of return to China, and suggest a form of government that is completely unacceptable to China. The British would be shocked if a Chinese governor were to arrive in Northern Ireland and dictate terms for its liberation from the United Kingdom. But they see nothing absurd in what they are doing in Hong Kong. The British, like many in the West, feel that they have a right to dictate terms to Asians.

Eventually, as East Asia becomes more affluent, the discussions will take place from a position of equality. But forums like ours can anticipate this by trying to create a form of discourse in which we approach each other with mutual respect.

Principle No. 2: Economic development
The fundamental concern of Western proponents of human rights is to remove egregious abuses and improve the living conditions of the

4.3 billion people who live outside the developed world. Let me suggest that the current Western campaign (even if it is rigorously carried out, which it is unlikely to be) will make barely a dent on the lives of the 4.3 billion people, although there will be symbolic victories like the Aquino revolution and the award of the Nobel Peace Prize to Aung San Suu Kyi.

There is only one force that has the power to "liberate" the Third World. Economic development is probably the most subversive force created in history. It shakes up old social arrangements and paves the way for the participation of a greater percentage of society in social and political decisions. The Chinese Communist Party can no longer regain the tight totalitarian control it enjoyed in Mao Zedong's time. Deng Xiaoping's reforms have killed that possibility. Hence, if the West wants to bury forever Mao's totalitarian arrangements, it should support Deng's reforms to the hilt, even if he has to occasionally crack down to retain political control. The fundamental trend is clear. It is, therefore, not surprising that three and a half years after Tiananmen, it is the "soft" and not the "hard" authoritarians who are in charge in Beijing. Clearly, if the Clinton administration wants to fulfil its goal of moving China towards a greater respect for human rights, it should do all in its power to accelerate China's economic development, not retard it.

Unfortunately, the promotion of economic development (unlike the promotion of democracy and human rights) is difficult. It has significant costs, direct and indirect, for developed societies. What may be good for the Third World (promoting economic development) would prove painful for Western societies in the short run. The EC, the United States and Japan, for example, would have to abandon their massive agricultural subsidies. Unfortunately (and paradoxically), the very nature of Western democratic societies (which inhibits politicians from speaking about sacrifices) may well be one of the biggest barriers to the effective spread of democracy and human rights in the Third World, including Asia.

Principle No. 3: Working with existing governments

Westerners should not even dream of overthrowing most of the existing governments in Asia. I say this because I was present at a lynching in Harvard University, the lynching of the Indonesian government. This was at a forum organised at the Kennedy School of Government to discuss the unfortunate killings in Dili in November 1991. Two of the American journalists who had had a close shave in the incident were there to present vivid firsthand accounts and whip up the crowd to a frenzy, with the help of a few leftist critics of the Indonesian government. This left a hapless State Department official to explain why the United States should continue working with the Suharto government. If the people in that room had had the power to depose the Indonesian government, they would have done it instantly, without paying a thought to the horrendous consequences that might follow. This is the attitude of many human rights activists: get rid of the imperfect governments we know—do not worry about the consequences that may follow. On their own, such activists will probably cause little trouble. But when they get into positions of influence, their ability to cause real damage increases by leaps and bounds.

In dealing with Asia, I am calling on the United States to take the long view. These are societies that have been around hundreds, if not thousands, of years. They cannot be changed overnight, even if, for example, Fang Lizhi is elected president of China. The experience of President Aquino should provide a vivid lesson to those who believe that one change at the top can reform everything.

What Asia needs at its present stage of development are governments that are committed to rapid economic development. Fortunately, these are quite a few, ranging across a wide political spectrum, from the communist societies of China and Vietnam, the military-dominated societies of Thailand and Indonesia to the democratic societies of South Korea, Taiwan and Malaysia. All are experiencing rapid economic growth. They should be rewarded and encouraged (if only to act as models for others). Sporadic instances of political crackdowns should be criticised, but these governments should not be penalised as long as their people's lives are improving. Only societies like North Korea and Myanmar, which have let their people stagnate for decades, deserve such disapproval.

Principle No. 4: Establishing minimal codes of civilised conduct

To a Western human rights activist, the suggestion that he should be a little moderate in making human rights demands on non-Western societies seems almost as absurd as the notion that a woman can be partially pregnant. In psychological attitudes, such an activist is no different from a religious crusader of a previous era. He demands total conversion and nothing else. Such activists can do a lot of damage with their zealotry. Unfortunately, since they occupy the high moral ground in Western societies, no government or media representative dares to challenge them openly. But some of the demands of these human rights activists would be unacceptable under any conditions. Most Asian societies would be shocked by the sight of gay rights activists on their streets. And, in most of them, if popular referendums were held, they would vote overwhelmingly in favour of the death penalty as well as censorship of pornography.

However, both Asians and Americans are human beings. They can agree on minimal standards of civilised behaviour that both would like to live by. For example, there should be no torture, no slavery, no arbitrary killings, no disappearances in the middle of the night, no shooting down of innocent demonstrators, no imprisonment without careful review. These rights should be upheld not only for moral reasons. There are sound functional reasons. Any society that is at odds with its best and brightest and shoots them down when they demonstrate peacefully, as Myanmar did, is headed for trouble. Most Asian societies do not want to be in the position that Myanmar is in today, a nation at odds with itself.

Principle No. 5: Letting the free press fly on its own wings

Finally, on the difficult issue of the freedom of the press, let me suggest that neither the West in general nor the United States in particular should take on the self-appointed role of guardian of free press in societies around the globe. Let each society decide for itself whether it would help or hinder its development if it decided to have a free press.

I have yet to meet an American who has any doubts about the virtues of having a free press. Even those who despise most journalists as the scum of the earth would not have it any other way. The value of the freedom of the press is absolute and unchallenged. The paradox here is that while they believe the virtues of a free press to be self-evident, they show no hesitation in ramming this concept down the throats of societies that are not enamoured by it.

Over time, a Darwinian process will establish whether societies with a free press will outperform those without one. So far, the record of the 20th century shows that societies that have free newspapers, such as the *New York Times* or the *Washington Post,* have outperformed societies with the *Pravda* and *Izvestia.* This winning streak may well continue. And if it does, more and more societies will naturally gravitate to social and political systems that can handle a totally free press, in the belief and hope that they will join the league of winners in the Darwinian contest between societies.

But let these decisions be made autonomously by these societies. There need be no fear that they will remain ignorant of the virtues of the US media. The globe is shrinking. With the proliferation of satellite dishes in villages in India and Indonesia, the sky is shrinking too. CNN and BBC are available worldwide. The *International Herald Tribune* and the *Wall Street Journal* can be obtained practically anywhere around the globe. Let the merits of these papers speak for themselves. The US media should not resort to the strong arm of the US executive branch or the Congress to sell their virtues for them.

In short, live and let live. If the United States is convinced that its systems of human rights and freedom of the press are the best possible systems for any society around the globe, let the virtues of these systems speak for themselves. As in the world of ideas, if a social system has merits, it will fly on its own wings. If it does not, it will not. Most Asians now know enough of these systems to make their own choices. Let them do so in peace.

1. Kishore Mahbubani, "The West and the Rest", *The National Interest*, No. 28, Summer 1992, p. 10.
2. Melvin Richter, "Despotism", in *Dictionary of the History of Ideas*, edited by Philip P. Wiener, New York, Charles Scribner's Sons, 1973, p. 1.
3. Edward W. Said, *Covering Islam: How the Media and the Experts Determine How We See the Rest of the World*, New York, Pantheon Books, 1981, p. xvii.
4. Nancy Caldwell Sorel, "First Encounters: Josef Stalin and Winston Churchill", *The Atlantic Monthly*, November 1991, p. 141.
5. Max Weber, *Politics As a Vocation*, Philadelphia, Fortress Press, 1965, p. 49.
6. Ibid., p. 47.

THE DANGERS OF DECADENCE: WHAT THE REST CAN TEACH THE WEST

FOREIGN AFFAIRS, SEPTEMBER/OCTOBER 1993.

In the summer of 1993, Samuel P. Huntington published "The Clash of Civilizations?" in *Foreign Affairs*. A contradiction developed in the Western response to this essay: the intellectual establishment, by and large, denounced it, but the attention and debate it sparked suggested that Huntington had struck a resonant chord in Western minds. When *Foreign Affairs* asked me to contribute one of their published responses, I thought it was worth explaining again that even though the West was now beginning to feel threatened by the Rest, in reality it was the Rest that had more reason to feel threatened by the West. If I had to rewrite the essay today, I would, with hindsight, remove some of its sharper edges. But the essay served its purpose in pointing out that a different world view existed.

In key Western capitals there is a deep sense of unease about the future. The confidence that the West would remain a dominant force in the 21st century, as it has for the past four or five centuries, is giving way to a sense of foreboding that forces like the emergence of fundamentalist Islam, the rise of East Asia and the collapse of Russia and Eastern Europe could pose real threats to the West. A siege mentality is developing. Within these troubled walls, Samuel P. Huntington's essay "The Clash of Civilizations?" is bound to resonate. It will, therefore, come as a great surprise to many Westerners to learn that the rest of the world fears the West even more than the West fears it, especially the threat posed by a wounded West.

Huntington is right: power is shifting among civilisations. But when the tectonic plates of world history move in a dramatic fashion, as they do now, perceptions of these changes depend on where one stands. The key purpose of this essay is to sensitise Western audiences to the perceptions of the rest of the world.

The retreat of the West is not universally welcomed. There is still no substitute for Western leadership, especially American leadership. Sudden withdrawals of American support from Middle Eastern or Pacific allies, albeit unlikely, could trigger massive changes that no one would relish. Western retreat could be as damaging as Western domination.

By any historical standard, the recent epoch of Western domination, especially under American leadership, has been remarkably benign. One dreads to think what the world would have looked like if either Nazi Germany or Stalinist Russia had triumphed in what have been called the "Western civil wars" of the 20th century. Paradoxically, the benign nature of Western domination may be the source of many problems. Today most Western policymakers, who are children of this era, cannot conceive of the possibility that their own words and deeds could lead to evil, not good. The Western media aggravate this genuine blindness. Most Western journalists travel overseas with Western assumptions. They cannot understand how the West could be seen as anything but benevolent. CNN is not the solution. The same visual images transmitted simultaneously into living rooms across the globe can trigger opposing perceptions. Western living rooms applaud when cruise missiles strike Baghdad. Most living outside see that the West will deliver swift retribution to nonwhite Iraqis or Somalis but not to white Serbians, a dangerous signal by any standard.

THE ASIAN HORDES

Huntington discusses the challenge posed by Islamic and Confucian civilisations. Since the bombing of the World Trade Center, Americans have begun to absorb European paranoia about Islam, perceived as a force of darkness hovering over a virtuous Christian civilisation. It is ironic that the West should increasingly fear Islam when daily the Muslims are reminded of their own weakness. "Islam has bloody borders," Huntington says. But in all conflicts between Muslims and pro-Western forces, the Muslims are losing, and losing badly, whether they be Azeris, Palestinians, Iraqis, Iranians or Bosnian Muslims. With so much disunity, the Islamic world is not about to coalesce into a single force.

Oddly, for all this paranoia, the West seems to be almost deliberately pursuing a course designed to aggravate the Islamic world. The West protests the reversal of democracy in Myanmar, Peru or Nigeria, but not in Algeria. These double standards hurt. Bosnia has wreaked incalculable damage. The dramatic passivity of powerful European nations as genocide is committed on their doorstep has torn away the thin veil of moral authority that the West had spun around itself as a legacy of its recent benign era. Few can believe that the West would have remained equally passive if Muslim artillery shells had been raining down on Christian populations in Sarajevo or Srebrenica.

Western behaviour towards China has been equally puzzling. In the 1970s, the West developed a love affair with a China ruled by a regime that had committed gross atrocities during the Great Leap Forward and the Cultural Revolution. But when Mao Zedong's disastrous rule was followed by a far more benign Deng Xiaoping era, the West punished China for what, by its historical standards, was a minor crackdown: the Tiananmen incident.

Unfortunately, Tiananmen has become a contemporary Western legend, created by live telecasts of the crackdown. Beijing erred badly in its excessive use of firearms, but it did not err in its decision to crack down. Failure to quash the student rebellion could have led to political disintegration and chaos, a perennial Chinese nightmare. Western policymakers concede this in private. They are also aware of the dishonesty of some Western journalists: dining with student dissidents and even egging them on before reporting on their purported "hunger strike". No major Western journal has exposed such dishonesty or developed the political courage to say that China had virtually no choice in Tiananmen. Instead, sanctions were imposed, threatening China's modernisation. Asians see that Western public opinion—deified in Western democracy—can produce irrational consequences. They watch with trepidation as Western policies on China lurch to and fro, threatening the otherwise smooth progress of East Asia.

Few in the West are aware that the West is responsible for aggravating turbulence among the more than 2 billion people living in Islamic and Chinese civilisations. Instead, conjuring up images of the two Asian hordes that Western minds fear most—two forces that invaded Europe, the Muslims and the Mongols—Huntington posits a Confucian-Islamic connection against the West. American arms sales to Saudi Arabia do not suggest a natural Christian-Islamic connection. Neither should Chinese arms sales to Iran. Both are opportunistic moves, based not on natural empathy or civilisational alliances. The real tragedy of suggesting a Confucian-Islamic connection is that it obscures the fundamentally different nature of the challenge posed by these forces. The Islamic world will have great difficulty modernising. Until then its turbulence will spill over into the West. East Asia, including China, is poised to achieve parity with the West. The simple truth is that East and Southeast Asia feel more comfortable with the West.

This failure to develop a viable strategy to deal with Islam or China reveals a fatal flaw in the West: an inability to come to terms with the shifts in the relative weights of civilisations that Huntington well documents. Two key sentences in Huntington's essay, when put side by side, illustrate the nature of the problem: first, "In the politics of civilizations, the peoples and governments of non-Western civilization no longer remain the objects of history as targets of Western colonization but join the West as movers and shapers of history," and second, "The West in effect is using international institutions, military power and economic resources to run the world in ways that will maintain Western predominance, protect Western interests and promote Western political and economic values." This combination is a prescription for disaster.

Simple arithmetic demonstrates Western folly. The West has 800 million people; the rest make up almost 4.7 billion. In the national arena, no Western society would accept a situation where 15 percent of its population legislated for the remaining 85 percent. But this is what the West is trying to do globally.

Tragically, the West is turning its back on the Third World just when it can finally help the West out of its economic doldrums. The developing world's dollar output increased in 1992 more than that of North America, the European Community and Japan put together. Two-thirds of the increase in US exports has gone to the developing world. Instead of encouraging this global momentum by completing the Uruguay Round, the West is doing the opposite. It is trying to create barriers, not remove them. French Prime Minister Edouard Balladur tried to justify this move by saying bluntly in Washington that the "question now is how to organize to protect ourselves from countries whose different values enable them to undercut us."

THE WEST'S OWN UNDOING

Huntington fails to ask one obvious question: If other civilisations have been around for centuries, why are they posing a challenge only now? A sincere attempt to answer this question reveals a fatal flaw that has recently developed in the Western mind: an inability to conceive that the West may have developed structural weaknesses in its core value systems and institutions. This flaw explains, in part, the recent rush to embrace the assumption that history has ended with the triumph of the Western ideal: individual freedom and democracy would always guarantee that Western civilisation would stay ahead of the pack.

Only hubris can explain why so many Western societies are trying to defy the economic laws of gravity. Budgetary discipline is disappearing. Expensive social programs and pork-barrel projects multiply with little heed to costs. The West's low savings and investment rates lead to declining competitiveness vis-à-vis East Asia. The work ethic is eroding, while politicians delude workers into believing that they can retain high wages despite becoming internationally uncompetitive. Leadership is lacking. Any politician who states hard truths is immediately voted out. Americans freely admit that many of their economic problems arise from the inherent gridlock of American democracy. While the rest of the world is puzzled by these fiscal follies, American politicians and journalists travel around the world preaching the virtues of democracy. It makes for a curious sight.

The same hero-worship is given to the idea of individual freedom. Much good has come from this idea. Slavery ended. Universal franchise followed. But freedom does not only solve problems; it can also cause them. The United States has undertaken a massive social experiment, tearing down social institution after social institution that restrained the individual. The results have been disastrous. Since 1960 the US population has increased 41 percent while violent crime has risen by 560 percent, single-mother births by 419 percent, divorce rates by 300 percent, and the percentage of children living in single-parent homes by 300 percent. This is massive social decay. Many a society shudders at the prospect of this happening on its shores. But instead of travelling overseas with humility, Americans confidently preach the virtues of unfettered individual freedom, blithely ignoring the visible social consequences.

The West is still the repository of the greatest assets and achievements of human civilisation. Many Western values explain the spectacular advance of mankind: the belief in scientific inquiry, the search for rational solutions, and the willingness to challenge assumptions. But a belief that a society is practising these values can lead to a unique blindness: the inability to realise that some of the values that come with this package may be harmful. Western values do not form a seamless web. Some are good. Some are bad. But one has to stand outside the West to see this clearly and to see how the West is bringing about its relative decline by its own hand. Huntington, too, is blind to this.

THE END OF AN EPOCH

TEXT OF SPEECH AT NATIONAL UNIVERSITY OF SINGAPORE CONVOCATION
CEREMONY. 1 SEPTEMBER 1993.

In September 1993 I was asked to speak at the convocation ceremony of the National University of Singapore, my alma mater. Most graduation speeches try to prepare the graduates for their next journey. My speech tried to do so too. I alerted the graduates that we were coming to the end of a 500-year cycle of the domination of the globe by Western civilisation. This was an amazingly bold claim to make by someone who did not have the credentials of a Toynbee. It could have been ignored or rebutted. Surprisingly, the *International Herald Tribune* took note of it and republished most of the text in an Op-Ed piece on 6 September 1993. History may yet reveal this essay to have been a little ahead of its time. But the era predicted in this essay will surely come.

Mr Pro-Chancellor, Graduates, Ladies and Gentlemen:

I have graduated twice—in 1971 from this university and in 1976 from Dalhousie University, Canada. But I have never participated in a convocation ceremony. In 1971 I developed chickenpox, and in 1976 I thought Canada was too far to return to for a convocation ceremony. I thank you for allowing me to experience the sweet pleasures of a convocation ceremony at my advanced age.

There is a palpable sense in this room that you have come to the end of a long road. Most of you are aware that an equally long journey awaits you. Most convocation speeches are about how you should prepare for your next journey. I will not disappoint you, but I may surprise you with my message. My theme is a simple one. You have spent many years in deep learning. To prepare yourself for your next journey, you may have to engage in some unlearning.

I cannot foretell the future. No one can. But if my hunch is correct, with the arrival of the 21st century we are probably going to move into the period of greatest historical change the world has seen. We are coming to the end of a 500-year cycle of global domination by Western civilisation. You must be aware that the West was basically confined to the European continent until the 15th or 16th century. Then came the greatest civilisation explosion seen in the history of man. The Portuguese, a tiny insignificant people today, went around the world, establishing colonies in South America, Africa and Asia. They were followed by the Spanish, the Dutch, the French and finally the British, who established the most far-flung empire ever seen in the history of man. The Germans came too late and never really developed strong colonial muscle.

As a consequence of this global explosion, despite the end of colonialism, the West has left its traces in every corner of the world, almost without exception. Contemporary South American culture and civilisation have European roots. The political boundaries of Africa today were drawn by Europeans. Australia, New Zealand, Canada and the United States are the descendants of Anglo-Saxon civilisation.

Virtually all of Asia was either colonised or invaded. Even Japan, the most successful Asian society so far, aspires mainly to be a member of the Western club. This global impact is no mean feat. In retrospect, it is amazing that the few hundred million people living in Europe could touch billions of lives. It was a historic achievement. It will take historians centuries to understand why this happened.

But all good things come to an end. Europe has finally become tired. The sheer effort of maintaining global empires and influence has finally exhausted the continent. Nothing demonstrates this more vividly than the inability of this mighty continent to put out a fire burning on its very own doorstep, the fire in Bosnia. The tragedy of Bosnia is not only about Serbs, Croats and Bosnian Muslims. It is fundamentally about the curtain falling on the greatest act of history.

As this curtain falls, a new drama will emerge. It would be foolish for me to pretend that I know what is going to come. Let me stress that I do not. But what I would like to provide you with are a few clues about what to expect. The first clue is that instead of the end of history, we will see the return of history. A clear signal of the foolishness that had engulfed many in the West was their infatuation with an essay that suggested that history was ending with the triumph of the Western idea. Instead, we will see the retreat of the Western idea as old and rich civilisations regain their self-confidence to discover their own roots. They will not shake off all that the West has given them. But they will learn to be selective in keeping Western ideas.

Many of you will be excited at this prospect of living through a period of enormous historical change, as you should be. But I should also prepare you for a certain confusion. Perhaps the best way to do that would be to compare your lives with mine. I was born in 1948 in Singapore, a British colony then. When I was in primary school, we were bussed to the Istana to wave the British flag, sing *God Save the Queen* and welcome the British governor-general to Singapore. One of my primary school classmates said to me then that when he grew up, he wanted to go to London. I asked him why. He answered—and I quote his words exactly—"Because the streets there must be paved with gold."

Looking at London today, it seems strange that a young boy in the 1950s could harbour such beliefs. But as London's fortunes ebbed, another city rose to take its place: Washington, DC. When I was posted there in 1982, 11 years ago, I went there with the clear sense that I was going to the Rome of the 20th century. And that it was. Every major global decision had to be examined or ratified by Washington, DC (together with the lesser Rome of that time, Moscow). But at the rate things are moving today, it is doubtful that Washington, DC will be the Rome of the 21st century.

What does all this mean for you? Let me answer with an analogy. Just imagine that you have been training for three to four years to sail across a mighty ocean. One of the basic instruments you are taught to rely on is a compass. Each time the compass needle faithfully points to the North Pole, you can tell which direction you are headed in because there is a clear point of reference you can orient yourselves against. But what happens when, after you have set out to sea, you discover that your compass no longer works? The North Pole has disappeared. There is no single point of reference to guide you.

One practical consequence of all this for you is that you may have to change some of the mental maps you inherited from your textbooks and from newspapers and television. Banish the thought that answers to critical global questions can be found only in New York, London or Paris. They are equally likely to be found in Shanghai or Tokyo, Jakarta or Bombay, or perhaps even Singapore.

It may seem unfair to you that I should spoil the sweet pleasures of graduation with this sombre message. Perhaps things may not prove to be so difficult after all. Perhaps both you and Singapore will experience smooth sailing in the years to come. If you do, I hope you will happily forget what I have said today. But if you do not experience smooth waters, I hope you will feel that you were at least mentally prepared for that possibility. As any sailor will tell you, he who can anticipate the next strong current or the next strong gust wins the race. I hope you will all win the races you are embarking on, and I wish you the very best as you set sail.

THE ASIA-PACIFIC

JAPAN ADRIFT

FOREIGN POLICY, NUMBER 88, FALL 1992.

When I took a sabbatical at the Center for International Affairs in Harvard University in 1991–92, I was required to write a thesis on any subject of my choice. I chose to write on Japan, a country that had always fascinated me. As the first Asian country to enter the developed world, Japan is greatly admired by all Asians. Curiously, it is also a country that has great difficulties coming to terms with its Asian neighbours. When the Cold War ended, Japan lost its natural moorings as the key ally of the United States in Northeast Asia. It had to find a new role and identity for itself in the post-Cold War era. Even though this essay was written in 1992, the central theme remains valid six years later. Japan is still adrift in the increasingly fluid geo-strategic environment of East Asia. This essay may help to explain why.

A Japanese folk tale tells of a young boy who lives in a coastal rice-farming village. One autumn morning, walking alone to work in the fields, he sees, to his horror, an approaching tsunami, which he knows will destroy the village. Knowing that he has no time to run down the hill to warn the villagers, he sets the rice fields on fire, sure that the desire to save their crops will draw all the villagers up the hill. The precious rice fields are sacrificed, but the villagers are saved from the tsunami. In what follows, some of the precious rice fields of strategic discourse in East Asia might burn, but in the process I hope to alert readers to the wave of change that approaches the region.

Most believe that Japan emerged from the Cold War a winner. As former Senator Paul Tsongas put it during his presidential campaign: "The Cold War is over and the Japanese won." The burst of the Japanese financial bubble in mid-1992 has somewhat undercut the power of that claim, but no one suggests that the Cold War's end has hurt Japan. Yet, in reality, Japan leaves the Cold War era more troubled than satisfied, more threatened than secure.

Japanese strategic planners can point to many gains at the end of the Cold War. The Soviet threat has all but disappeared. The chances of a major war either close to or involving Japan seem extremely low. China, which once overshadowed Japan, has since diminished in stature, especially after the June 1989 massacre at Tiananmen Square. The East Asian region, Japan's economic backyard, continues to prosper, boosted now by the economic takeoff of China's coastal provinces. Japan has emerged as the world's second largest economic power, with the prospect of overtaking the first, the United States, in a decade or two. Even in absolute terms, Japan already invests more for the future than does the larger United States.

Despite those significant gains, Japan now faces its most difficult, if not precarious, strategic environment since World War II. The Soviet threat that drew Japan comfortably into the Western camp and provided the glue for the US-Japanese security relationship is now gone. Neither the United States nor Japan, each for its own reasons, is yet prepared to abandon the Mutual Security Treaty (MST). But the strategic pillars upon which the MST rested have eroded, leaving the Japanese to wonder whether—and under what circumstances—the United States will be willing to come to Japan's defence in the future.

The notion of a strategically insecure economic superpower is hard to swallow. Consider this: During the Cold War, Japanese security planners did not even consider the possibility of a rupture in the US-Japanese security relationship. Now they do. If that tie breaks, Japan could find itself strategically vulnerable in the face of at least three potentially unfriendly, if not adversarial, neighbours: China, Korea and Russia. To be sure, no military conflicts are imminent between Japan and any one of them. No war planning is required. But whereas Japan and its neighbours did not worry about each other during the Cold War, now they do. A *Beijing Review* article in February 1992 warned, "Japan has become more active and independent in conducting its foreign policy in an attempt to fill the vacancy in the Asia-Pacific region left by the withdrawal of US and Russian influences." And South Korean planners say that even after reunification, US forces should stay in Korea to protect Korea from Japan.

The root cause of Japan's problems in the post-Cold War era is the troubled US-Japanese relationship. The key security interests, especially the containment of the Soviet Union, that held the two countries together have diminished or disappeared. It is astonishing how that simple point is either missed or ignored in the analysis of Japanese foreign policy. Consider, for example, how much US and Japanese interests have diverged over Russia. While the United States is trying to rescue Russia, Japan is not convinced that its national interests include helping Russia.

That divergence is significant. In the wake of World War II, and with the coming of the Korean War, the United States and Japan struck a bargain, albeit an implicit one. The United States forgave all that Japan had done in World War II, and in return Japan became a loyal and dependable ally against the communist bloc.

Although the new relationship was not forced upon Japan, it was a manifestly unequal one. In practical day-to-day terms, it functioned like the Lone Ranger-Tonto relationship. Many Japanese may be offended by the comparison, but the evidence is overwhelming. The roots of inequality go back to the very origins of the US-Japanese relationship, when Commodore Matthew Perry demanded that Japan open up to the world. That "demander-demandee" pattern has persisted for more than a century. The Japanese remember well President Franklin Roosevelt's implicit demand that Japan withdraw from China and Secretary of State John Foster Dulles's demand that Premier Yoshida Shigeru cease his efforts to normalise ties with China, both of which made President Richard Nixon's *shokku* decision to normalise ties with China—without consulting Japan—even more galling. Except on trade and economic issues, Japan has almost never said "no" to any significant US demand since World War II, especially in the area of international security. Japan has also served as a vital banker for US foreign policy goals, shaping its official development assistance policies to meet both US and Japanese needs. Its long history of submitting to US demands explains the appeal to the Japanese of Shintaro Ishihara's book *The Japan That Can Say No*, as well as the emergence of the new term *kenbei*, meaning dislike of the United States.

In recent times, Japan has hesitated only once in responding to an important US military demand, namely, that it contribute significantly to the Persian Gulf war. That hesitation was rooted in an expectation that Japan's oil supplies would not be affected by the Iraqi invasion of Kuwait, in a sense of surprise that the West could abandon Saddam Hussein so quickly after building him up as a Western asset, and in the Japanese public's aversion to direct participation in military conflict. That hesitation cost the Japanese dearly. Their reputation suffered badly in the United States. As a consequence, even Japan's payment of $13 billion, the largest single contribution from any non-Arab coalition member, did not alleviate the feeling that Japan had once again tried to be a free rider on the United States.

The decision of the US government to use the US media to pressure Japan publicly to supply some of the money, if not the men, to help in the Gulf War was a dangerous move on two counts. First, many Americans already feel threatened by Japan's growing economic power. As Harvard political scientist Samuel Huntington has put it, Americans are obsessed with Japan because they see it "as a major threat" to US primacy in a crucial arena of power: economics. Many Americans, therefore, ask a common-sense question: Why should the United States spend money to defend a "free-riding" economic competitor? The media attention, then, further eroded US support for the US-Japanese relationship. It also reinforced the growing Japanese consensus that Americans are making Japan the scapegoat for their own domestic economic troubles. Objective analysis supports the Japanese contention that the root causes of the United States' economic problems lie in the failure of the US government, in both the executive and legislative branches, to solve problems of its own creation: budget deficits, heavy internal and external borrowing, and the lack of sufficient long-term investment in either industry or the labour force, to cite just a few obvious points.

The admiration that the Japanese have genuinely felt for the United States, in part because it was unusually generous as an occupying power, is steadily diminishing. Japan is no longer prepared to be the "Tonto". In fact, the Japanese increasingly perceive themselves to be superior to the "Lone Ranger". Thus, a structural change—from one-way condescension to mutual condescension—is taking place in the psychological relationship between Japan and the United States.

To prevent a breakdown in US-Japanese relations, the Japanese establishment has consciously woven a thick web of economic interdependence between the two countries. However, even without a serious US-Japanese rift, Japan could find itself abandoned. Fuelled by perceptions of economic rivalry, US relations with Japan could become friendly but merely normal—like, for instance, US relations with Switzerland. The United States may then no longer feel obliged to defend Japan or maintain forces in East Asia to protect Japan's sea lanes. Alternatively, close relations could fall victim to a resurgence of US isolationism: "What we are concerned with is an America turning inward, politically and economically," said Takakazu Kuriyama, the Japanese ambassador to the United States. The Japanese fear that continued US economic troubles—exacerbated by the US government's inability to deal with them—would make Americans unwilling and unable to pay for a continued US military overseas.

DIFFICULT NEIGHBOURS

Deprived of the US nuclear umbrella, Japan, the only country in the world to have experienced a nuclear attack, will feel threatened by its nuclear-equipped neighbours. What should the Japanese Self-Defence Forces do if China implements its new law on the disputed Senkaku Islands and places troops there? Could a Chinese force be removed as easily as the symbolic Taiwanese presence was a few years ago? With its powerful economy, Japan currently towers over China, Korea and Russia, but each raises unique security concerns. A hostile alliance of any two of those would be a strategic nightmare for a solitary Japan. With the new sense of uncertainty about the future viability of the US-Japanese defence relationship, Japan has to take a fresh look at its relations with those three neighbours.

Of the three relationships, the Russo-Japanese one appears to be the most troubled at present. The unresolved issue of the Kuril Islands continues to bedevil relations, but the troubled history of relations between Japan and Russia—including the brutal Soviet treatment of Japanese POWs and the USSR's last-minute entry into World War II against Japan in violation of the treaty both had signed—aggravates Japanese distrust of the Russians. Even if the Kuril dispute is resolved, Japan has to ask itself whether long-term Japanese interests would be served by helping Russia become strong again.

Given the economic, social and political mess that it finds itself in, Russia is not likely to threaten Japan in the near future; but a continuing cool Japanese attitude towards Russia could lead to problems with Japan's Western allies. In May 1992 German Chancellor Helmut Kohl publicly criticised Japan for not doing more to help Russia. The triumphant visit of Russian President Boris Yeltsin to Washington in June 1992 indicated that the United States is moving even closer to Russia. How long can Japan, a nominal member of the Western camp, buck that trend?

Traditionally, the Japanese have viewed Korea as a "dagger pointed at the heart of Japan". In the past, they have not hesitated to intervene in or invade Korea, leaving behind a rich residue of Korean distrust of Japan. Remarkably, 47 years after World War II, the Japanese have not even begun to reduce that distrust.

During the Cold War, Japan did not have to worry about Korea. The two large Korean armies threatened each other, not Japan. But if Korea reunifies, the succeeding Korean state, like united Germany, would inherit a formidable military capability, and it would be situated within striking distance of Japan. In 1992 the prospects of an early reunification do not look good—at least not until North Korean leader Kim Il Sung dies. But the outlines of the likely solution to the Korean problem are becoming clear. South Korea is likely to emerge as the successor state of the two Koreas, as West Germany did in reunified Germany.

The two powers that have guaranteed North Korean independence now show less interest in the continued division of Korea. Russia, as demonstrated by Mikhail Gorbachev's behaviour, now even has a vested interest in a unified Korea, under South Korea, because that could enable Russia to play the "Korea card" against Japan. China's interests are not so clear-cut. The regime in Beijing is probably not keen to see the disappearance of another ideological ally (although visitors to Beijing and Pyongyang can testify that those two cities seem to be in different ideological universes). However, the Chinese are remarkably pragmatic in their foreign policy. The Chinese concept of "flexible power" (*quan bian*) predates Machiavelli by centuries. If China's long-term interests favour a unified Korean peninsula, China will not hesitate to abandon an ideological ally. Japan should, therefore, assume that a unified Korea—with all the potential dangers that could bring—is in the making, even though the South Koreans, having watched West Germany's difficulties, favour a slower process of reunification.

Currently, the Japanese are obsessed, and correctly so, with the threat that North Korea will develop nuclear weapons. They would not feel any less alarmed if South Korea inherited a nuclear capability. Given the traditional Japanese-Korean antipathies, several Japanese officials have confidentially said that while Japan can live with a nuclear-armed Russia and China, a nuclear-armed Korea would be unacceptable. Almost certainly, Japan would build its own nuclear weapons in response.

The North Korean nuclear issue illustrates the complexity of the Northeast Asian security environment. The campaign against North Korea's nuclear development is publicly led by the United States and Japan. Yet China probably realises that a North Korean nuclear capability could trigger the nuclearisation of Japan. China knows that it cannot stop Japan from going nuclear on its own, and, more crucially, it knows that only the United States can. Hence, even though China in principle opposes the US military presence in the region, there is nothing that it dreads more than a US military withdrawal that could induce Japan to acquire its own nuclear weapons.

Of the three, the most difficult relationship for Japan to work out ultimately in the post-Cold War era will be that with China. Unlike Russia, China cannot be treated purely as an adversary. Yet, with the disappearance of the Soviet threat and the perception that the United States may be turning inwards, both China and Japan are beginning to wonder whether they may not be left as the only two giant wrestlers in the ring. Both have already begun to circle each other warily, each trying to ascertain the other's intentions.

For China, the emergence of Japan has probably come as an unpleasant surprise. After Japan's surrender in World War II, its adoption of the peace constitution and its servile dedication to US foreign policy, China did not perceive Japan either as a threat or as an equal. With its nuclear capability, its permanent seat on the United Nations Security Council and the assiduous courtship it enjoyed from the United States and other Western countries during the Cold War, China clearly felt itself to be superior to Japan. It blithely ignored Japan's growing economic strength. Neither during Mao's lifetime nor after did China try to work out a long-term *modus vivendi* with Japan. Instead, its policies towards Japan have been offshoots of China's other concerns, using Japan to escape international isolation in the 1950s and again in the wake of Tiananmen.

Japan does not relish the idea of coming to terms with China on a one-to-one basis. For most of the Cold War, Japan looked up to China. Both Japan's surrender in World War II, and the traditional relationship, in which Japan was a cultural and political satellite of China, made it easy for the Japanese to accept an unequal position. Today, however, they no longer revere China, perhaps not even culturally. Japanese leaders and officials have to disguise their disdain for China. They are especially contemptuous of the fact that more than 100 years after the Meiji Restoration of 1868, when Japan began to institute reforms to meet the challenge of a technologically superior Western civilisation, China still has not come to terms with the modern world.

In the short run, Japan is primarily concerned that instability in China could bring a mass of refugees to Japan, the beginnings of which the Japanese have already experienced with the arrival of small Chinese fishing vessels. In the long run, it fears that a successful China could once again overshadow Japan. Although at present the prospects for that do not look good, the Japanese recognise with awe the creativity and dynamism of Chinese scientists and entrepreneurs outside China. They see the birth of a new economic synergy linking Hong Kong and Taiwan to China. They realise that a well-organised China could leave Japan trailing, as the Tang dynasty did.

China holds the key to the solution of many of the region's pressing problems, such as those in Korea, Indochina and Taiwan. Yet, despite some common interests, Japan will probably find it unwise to raise those issues—except perhaps for Korea—with China. China would reject any discussion on Taiwan, which it considers to be an internal issue. The Chinese leadership would be deeply alarmed if a reduced US presence in Asia brought closer political relations between Japan and Taiwan. So far, however, Japan has behaved with exquisite political correctness on the issue of Taiwan.

The Indochina issue illustrates the difficulty of working out a new Sino-Japanese *modus vivendi*. The Soviet collapse paved the way for the symbolic re-capitulation of Vietnam to China. China felt that it had reasserted its historical influence over the Indochinese peninsula. China, however, is in no position to help Vietnam extricate itself from its economic mess. Japan could help, but China would be deeply troubled by the prospect that Vietnam (or any Southeast Asian state) might be transformed into an economic satellite of Japan.

The potential for Sino-Japanese misunderstanding is great. As long as Beijing remains relatively isolated, it will probably not do anything to provoke Japan. However, that relatively calm state of affairs may not last forever. China could emerge out of the cloud of Tiananmen. Japan's economic influence in the region could become even more pronounced. In the hope of "containing" that influence on China's periphery, some Chinese planners have already begun to think of a "small triangle"—composed of the United States, Japan and China—to replace the "big triangle", which consisted of the United States, the USSR and China. A new power structure is thus in the making. Despite the clear evidence that Japan will face new challenges in its relations with the United States and its neighbours, it will be psychologically difficult for the Japanese to admit that they face a problematic new strategic environment. They feel no immediate pain at the end of the Cold War. Instead, Japan appears to have been catapulted to a position of global eminence. Few greater gatherings of luminaries have been seen in recent times than at Emperor Hirohito's funeral.

THE FORCES OF DRIFT

Even if the Japanese were to recognise the new challenges before them, five powerful forces will encourage continued drift.

First, restructuring the US-Japanese relationship will be difficult. There is a great mismatch of needs, attitudes, perceptions and power relations. Japan needs the United States for its security; the United States does not need Japan. Since Commodore Perry's time, the United States has been used to making demands on Japan. Japan has never reciprocated. The Japanese see theirs as a tiny country overshadowed by a giant United States. But the American public also increasingly sees the Japanese as larger than life, providing the only real threat to continued US economic predominance. Racial differences aggravate that sense of threat. The power imbalance can be demonstrated with an analogy. Washington sees the US-Japanese relationship as a friendly game of chess. But where Washington sees it as a one-to-one game, Tokyo sees three other players on the same chessboard: China, Korea and Russia. Any Japanese move against the United States affects its ties with the other three. In Japanese eyes, there is no "level playing field" in the game.

Superficially, there would appear to be no trouble in the security sphere. The United States has never expressed any doubts about its commitment to the MST, notwithstanding the ongoing question of the cost of keeping US troops in Japan. There is no American public debate on the treaty. "Why risk change?" is the attitude of Japanese policymakers. To restructure the relationship, Japan will have to persuade the United States to continue to protect Japan and at the same time demand that the United States treat Japan as an equal partner. Asking for protection and parity in the same breath is never easy. It will be equally difficult for both sides to admit that while the form of the defence relationship will remain the same (meaning the MST will not be changed), the substance will be different. Instead of protecting Japan from the vanished Soviet threat, the treaty will restrain the nuclearisation and militarisation of Japan, consequently reassuring Japan's neighbours that it will remain peaceful. In short, the main purpose of the US-Japanese MST will be to contain Japan's growth as a military power. The key problem will be, of course, arriving at such an understanding clearly and publicly, so that the American body politic understands and supports the MST, but without offending the Japanese people.

Second, if the Japanese admit to themselves that they face a new strategic environment with the long-term US defence commitment in doubt, they fear that the only obvious alternative to the MST is an independent Japanese military—and nuclear—capability. Japan is by no means a military midget. Its current defensive military capability is respected. However, without a nuclear umbrella and strong offensive capabilities, Japan cannot contemplate military confrontation with its nuclear-equipped neighbours. Some Japanese desire an independent nuclear capability, but they know that would set off global alarm bells. Many in the West have already developed an inferiority complex with regard to the Japanese and would be deeply troubled to see Japan extend its economic superiority into the military field. The West is not ready to accept the possibility that the pre-eminent power in all fields could be a non-Western country like Japan, even though Japan is nominally a member of the "Western" group.

Third, if Japan tries to shift course and move closer to its neighbours, it would have to abandon a century-old policy of believing that Japan's destiny lies with the West. Yukichi Fukuzawa, the great Meiji-era reformer, said that Japan should "escape from Asia, and enter into Europe". If it now reverses course and "enters" into Asia, some tensions could also develop with its Western partners. For example, at the end of the Cold War, the promotion of democracy and human rights has been elevated in the Western scheme of priorities. Japan has gone along, by and large, though more out of convenience than conviction. However, as the West applies those new policies pragmatically on strategically important countries (Algeria, for example), and less pragmatically on less vital countries, the difference in geographical interests between Japan and the West will surface. Knowing well that a policy strongly based on the promotion of human rights would only invite several Asian countries to drag out Japan's record up to the end of World War II, Japan is caught between the devil and the deep blue sea in trying to balance its interests as a "Western" and as an Asian country. Hence one more reason for drifting along.

Fourth, in order to review and reform its relations with its three neighbours, Japan will have to confront ghosts from the past that it has consciously ignored since World War II. To reshape its relations with both China and Korea, Japan must be able to look them squarely in the eye and acknowledge that it was responsible for some of the most painful chapters in their histories. Without such an acknowledgement, it is hard to imagine how new bonds of trust can be forged. The Japanese have so far carefully and circumspectly expressed "regret" and "contrition", but unlike the Germans, they have not yet brought themselves to apologise directly to those peoples.

As long as Emperor Hirohito was living, many Japanese felt constrained in discussing the issue of war crimes because they wanted to avoid embarrassing him. The US decision to ignore the atrocities committed by the Japanese during World War II in order to gain a strong ally in the Korean War aggravated the natural tendency to avoid facing a painful topic. Many Japanese also feel that what Japan did in Korea and China was no different from what Western colonisers did elsewhere, that the rape of Nanking was no different from the British massacre of Indian protesters at Amritsar. Why, they ask, should Japan atone for its colonial sins when the West never did so? But the Japanese ability to win the trust of their neighbours is linked to their own ability to acknowledge what happened. Many Japanese see a conspiracy to blacken Japan's name in the renewed discussion of World War II. They do not realise that it is an inevitable consequence of Japanese success. If Japan had remained like Bangladesh, few would be interested in discussing its past. With its growing influence, however, it is natural that Japan's neighbours need reassurances that its newfound power will be exercised benignly.

Fifth, in attempting to chart a new course, Japan would also have to face its built-in cultural and political limitations. The Japanese have created a fairly harmonious society, but it is ethnocentric and exclusive. A foreigner has virtually no hope of being accepted as an equal member, no matter how "Japanese" he or she may become in behaviour. The inability (or unwillingness) of the Japanese to absorb the several hundred thousand Koreans who have lived in Japan for generations is a powerful statement of the exclusivity of Japanese society. Ethnic exclusivity, as demonstrated by South Africa, does not foster good neighbourliness.

Those cultural obstacles are compounded by Japan's weak, divided and scandal-ridden political leadership. The frequent changes of prime ministers, the appointment of weak individuals to senior political positions, and the absence of visionary leaders for the new times have all compounded the country's inertia. Japanese behaviour at Asia-Pacific Economic Cooperation Council meetings illustrates the problem. Unlike all the others, the Japanese delegation arrives with two heads, one from the Ministry of International Trade and Industry and one from the Foreign Ministry. While it is not unusual for international delegations to include multiple agencies, it is unusual for one national delegation to speak with two voices. As a result, Japanese policy is often deadlocked, and the signals it sends are often mixed and confusing.

A NEW REGIONAL ARCHITECTURE

Despite these five reasons why Japan is likely to drift along, there are equally strong pressures upon Japan to set a bold new course in its foreign policy. The creation of a plethora of new committees, in both the ruling Liberal Democratic Party and the Parliament, demonstrates a new effervescence in Japanese thinking.

Japan's position as an "economic giant" but a "political dwarf" is no longer viable. Japan's economy is already larger than all other East Asian economies combined, and the Japanese gross national product (GNP) makes up 70 percent of the total for all of Asia, not counting the former Soviet republics. No European country enjoys such a position in its neighbourhood. Only the United States comes close, in the size of its GNP compared to the Latin American economies. Yet, Japan has relatively little political influence in East Asia—much less than the United States has in Latin America. To understand the anomalous position of Japan in East Asia, imagine the United States having less political influence in Latin America than either Brazil or the countries of the Andean Pact do. That is Japan's current position in East Asia in relation to China or the Association of South-East Asian Nations (ASEAN). That situation cannot endure.

Japan's problem is that it must create a new political architecture for the region—from scratch. History does not help. The only traditional precolonial political architecture of the region rested on the concept of the "Middle Kingdom", whereby East and Southeast Asia paid tribute to Beijing. Japan cannot recreate such an arrangement. Nor can China, given its current weakness. In forging a new architecture, Japan will find that it must construct at least five pillars.

The first pillar must be a reaffirmation of Japan's non-nuclear status. Japanese leaders may privately consider it unfair that Japan is still not trusted with nuclear weapons, yet they know that Japan's decision to acquire nuclear weapons would destabilise all of its gains since World War II: Japan would find itself isolated not just from its three neighbours but also from the West. That would be nothing short of a strategic nightmare. A strong (rather than grudging) reaffirmation of the non-nuclear option would enhance its neighbours' confidence that Japan's intentions are peaceful. In this light, the continuing rejection of militarism by the Japanese public should also be seen as a strength rather than a weakness because it assuages the fears of Japan's neighbours.

The second pillar of the new architecture must be a restructured US-Japanese relationship. Fundamentally, Japan has to ask itself whether allowing the US-Japanese relationship to drift on its present course will naturally lead to stronger and closer bonds between the two countries or whether the continuation of the present pattern—in which the Japanese public feels constantly bullied by the United States and the American public sees Japan as a "free rider" growing wealthy at the United States' expense—will bring a progressive deterioration.

So far, Japan has concentrated its efforts on enhancing the economic interdependence between the two countries, acting as a banker for US foreign policy, accepting US vetoes of Japanese foreign policy initiatives, and making it affordable for the Pentagon to station military forces in Japan by paying half the cost. In private, the Japanese often see the United States as a temperamental bull that has to be appeased from time to time. But since the US government has expressed no desire to change the relationship, Japanese planners might wonder, why risk change? Yet, the Japanese need to be aware of the profoundly democratic nature of American society. The commitment of the US government to defend Japan is real only if it has the support of the American people. Japan cannot afford to make the same mistake the South Vietnamese generals did in 1975, when they accepted at face value Washington's commitment to defend Saigon without paying attention to American public opinion.

Today, Japan has to convince both the US government and the American people that the US-Japanese security relationship is in the interest of both countries; that Japan is no free rider; and that its commitment to a non-nuclear strategy serves the interests of the United States, the West and the region. After all, if the United States abandons the MST, US defence planners will have many new concerns. If Japan goes nuclear, the United States will have to plan a defence against a nuclear power that, unlike the USSR, could be technologically more advanced than the United States. Japan could also pose new competition for American arms exporters, an area Japan has not ventured into so far.

The economic tensions between the two countries must also be addressed squarely. The United States has to publicly admit that Japan is being made the scapegoat for the former's inability to get its own economic house in order. For its part, Japan needs to make a major pronouncement that a strong United States is in the interest of Japan and the Asia-Pacific region as a whole and that it will work with its neighbours in formulating economic policies to enhance both US competitiveness and US economic interests in the region. Such a bold announcement, followed by concrete actions, may help lay to rest a growing sentiment in the United States that Japan is weakening the US economy.

There is a seeming contradiction between Japan's need for continued US protection and its desire to stand up for itself. But that contradiction arises out of the peculiar nature of the US-Japanese relationship, in which a giant economic power is not allowed to have nuclear weapons. If Japan could become a nuclear power, it could behave like France or the United Kingdom towards the United States; but because that is not an option, the United States should allow Japan to spread its influence in other spheres and not remain a satellite of US foreign policy.

The third pillar of Japan's new architecture must be the development of "good neighbour" policies with China, Korea and Russia. Recent history in Western Europe has demonstrated that long-held animosities need not endure. While Britain, France and Germany first joined together under pressure of the common Soviet threat, they are now held together by the immensely intricate networks forged between their societies. Japan can replicate such networks with its neighbours. Trade and investment flows are leading the way; in their wake the Japanese should seek to foster greater cross-cultural understanding. Southeast Asia has long been described as the Balkans of Asia. The many races, languages, cultures and religions approximate the Balkans in their variety; they have helped form a history that is equally complex and sad. Despite those obstacles, the ASEAN countries have managed to forge the most successful regional cooperation of the Third World. Tokyo can do no less if it undertakes bold initiatives such as resolving the islands dispute with Russia and apologising to the Korean and Chinese peoples for the horrors of the past. The Japanese have great psychological difficulties in accepting the need for an apology, but they should realise that just as they will never be able to trust the Russians until Moscow apologises for the brutal treatment of Japanese POWs after World War II, so their neighbours feel the same way about Tokyo.

The fourth pillar must be to build some sense of a common Asian home. Europe was able to escape the legacy of centuries of rivalries and animosities by creating a feeling of a common European home long before Gorbachev uttered that phrase, with a common Greco-Roman heritage serving as a foundation. The ultimate challenge faced by the Japanese is to try to achieve a similar sense in East Asia. Only a common perception that all are riding in the same boat will prevent the region from dissolving into bitter and dangerous conflict. Perhaps the decision of the Chinese, Japanese, Korean and other East Asian communities in Los Angeles to forget their differences and work together after the recent riots could have a demonstrative effect on their parent countries.

Creating such a sense of a common Asian home will be another difficult psychological shift for the Japanese. Ever since the Meiji Restoration, they have equated success with Western acceptance. Clearly, though, to earn the long-term trust of its Asian neighbours—especially giants like China, India and Indonesia—Japan has to demonstrate that it respects them as fellow Asian countries. It must not treat them with the condescension they sometimes encounter in the West. Japanese aid policies, for example, cannot be simple extensions of Western aid policies, if only because Japan has different geographical interests. In dealing with Asia, Japan has so far bent almost reflexively to US or Western interests, although neither the United States nor Japan will admit to any coercion. For example, when Malaysia suggested an East Asian economic grouping, Japan acquiesced to US opposition before considering whether the region would benefit from such an organisation. Similarly, following the Cambodian peace agreement, Japan wanted to lift its investment embargo on Vietnam and end the Asian Development Bank moratorium on loans to Vietnam. But here, too, it gave in to the US position.

The United States does not hesitate in making such demands on Japan, asserting its rights as a protector. Yet, wiser counsel should prevail in Washington. The United States should stop asking Japan to fashion its policies primarily to defend US interests; that will not work in the long run. US opposition to new multilateral links in the Asia-Pacific region clearly illustrates the short-sightedness of US policies. With the explosive growth in trade and investment among the East Asian societies, there is a great need for strengthened multilateral links to lubricate those contacts and provide venues for resolving common problems among the East Asian countries.

Any serious consideration of a common Asian home evokes great disquiet in the United States and in the West generally, mostly for fear that another exclusive racial club is being formed. That reflects Western ignorance of the enormous racial and cultural divisions within Asia. The main function of a common Asian home (to include Australia and New Zealand), like the common European home, would be to reduce or dissolve racial identities, not to enhance them.

Finally, the fifth pillar requires Japan to become a good global citizen. Japan's efforts to gain a permanent seat on the UN Security Council reflect that desire. However, its method of trying to gain that seat is a classic case of putting the cart before the horse. Without an established track record of managing international conflicts, what would Japan do on the Security Council? Japan's case for a permanent seat would clearly be enhanced if Tokyo could demonstrate, as the

United States has in the Middle East, that it can take the lead in resolving international conflicts.

Consider, for example, the Cambodian peace process. An excellent peace agreement has been signed, but its implementation has been hobbled by a lack of funding, with the United States finding it hard to raise its share of the cost of UN peacekeeping operations. Following traditional behaviour, the Japanese will wait for the US government to approach them for financial assistance and, after some hesitation, agree to the US request. Instead, the Japanese government should take the initiative and announce that it will meet any financial shortfall in the Cambodian UN operations, and take the lead in meeting the economic reconstruction needs of Cambodia. Japan should declare that it will ensure that the long nightmare of the Cambodian people is finally over, thus fulfilling its responsibilities to both the region and common humanity. The entire operation would cost Japan $1 or $2 billion, a fraction of what it paid for the Gulf War, yet the kudos that Japan could earn—in the region, in the West, and especially in the United States—would be enormous. Such a move could drastically alter public perceptions of the Japanese as mere calculating beings with no moral purpose. That is the sort of bold leap that Japan needs to make.

Bold steps, of course, have not been the hallmark of Japanese foreign policy since World War II. Caution has been the key word. But a new trans-Pacific crisis is in the making. Fortunately, both the dangers and the opportunities are equally clear. The East Asian region is experiencing perhaps the most spectacular economic growth in human history. It began with Japan and spread throughout the region. Yet, all East Asian governments realise that their countries' economic growth would still be crippled if Japan were to falter. Japan, therefore, has considerable influence in fashioning a new political architecture for the region. However, to succeed, it will have to meet the interests not only of Japan, but also of its three immediate neighbours, of the East Asian region generally, and of the United States. The future will severely test the diplomatic vision and skill of Japan's leaders.

"THE PACIFIC IMPULSE"

SURVIVAL, SPRING 1995.

In September 1994 I gave an opening address at the 36th Annual Conference of the International Institute of Strategic Studies held in Vancouver. The conference brings together mainly American and European strategic thinkers. The natural assumption in these strategic minds was that Europe was ahead of the rest of the world in strategic theory and practice, that the key concepts and paradigms had been worked out in Europe, and that the rest of the world could do no better than emulate Europe. My lecture shocked the audience on two counts: first, I suggested that the Asia-Pacific, not Europe, had better prospects for peace; second, I suggested that the ways of the Pacific may provide an alternative *Weltanschauung* for strategic thinkers. The response was clearly hostile. But when excerpts from my speech were published in *Foreign Affairs* (as "The Pacific Way") and *Survival* (as "The Pacific Impulse"), they drew a kinder response. Gareth Evans, the then Australian foreign minister, told me that he had quoted me in his speeches, especially my suggestion that the Asia-Pacific would unleash a burst of explosive creativity with the fusion of Asian and American civilisations.

The 21st century will see a struggle between an "Atlantic impulse" and a "Pacific impulse". For the past few centuries, the Atlantic impulse has determined the course of world history. If my assumptions are right and the Pacific impulse takes centre stage over the Atlantic impulse, then Eurocentric strategic analysts will have to rethink their concepts and assumptions to understand the future flow of history.

The 21st century will be unique because there will be three centres of world power (Europe, North America and East Asia) as opposed to two in the 20th century (Europe and North America) and one in the immediate preceding centuries (Europe). In previous centuries, Europe set the course of world history: it colonised most parts of the world, shook up other empires and societies (including China, Japan and Islam) and occupied relatively empty spaces (North America and Australasia) through immigration. The two World Wars of the 20th century, and even the Cold War succeeding them, were essentially pan-European struggles. East Asia, by contrast, had little impact on the rest of the world.

It would be dangerous for both Europe and mankind if analysts were unable to liberate themselves from Eurocentric conceptions of the world. Like all other parts of the world that have experienced greatness, Europe too is becoming exhausted. The time has come for other regions to contribute as much as Europe has in moving the world forward.

THE RISE OF EAST ASIA

In the 21st century, East Asia will shed its passivity. The region's sheer economic weight will give it a voice and a role. As recently as 1960, Japan and East Asia together represented 4 percent of the world's gross national product (GNP), while the United States, Canada and Mexico represented 37 percent. Today, both areas have a similar proportion of the world's GNP (some 23–24 percent), but, with more than half of the world's economic growth taking place in Asia in the 1990s, the North Atlantic Free Trade Agreement (NAFTA) and European economies will progressively become relatively smaller.[1] Initially, it will be the economic weight of East Asia that will have the most significant impact. This may explain why both European economists and industrialists treat East Asia with respect. By contrast, ideologues and strategists, seeing no vigorous intellectual challenge from East Asia, believe that they have little to learn from the region.

This may explain why almost all strategic analysts assume only the European experience can explain East Asia's future. And in all the inevitable comparisons with Europe, East Asia comes out second best. Richard Betts says, "one of the reasons for optimism about peace in Europe is the apparent satisfaction of the great powers with the status quo," while in East Asia there is "an ample pool of festering grievances, with more potential for generating conflict than during the Cold War, when bipolarity helped stifle the escalation of parochial disputes."[2]

Aaron L. Friedberg says: "While civil war and ethnic strife will continue for some time to smoulder along Europe's peripheries, in the long run it is Asia that seems far more likely to be the cockpit of great-power conflict. The half millennium during which Europe was the world's primary generator of war (as well as wealth and knowledge) is coming to a close. But, for better or for worse, Europe's past could be Asia's future."[3]

Barry Buzan and Gerald Segal, after reviewing the history of conflict in East Asia, say:

All of these historical legacies remain and, taken together, they suggest political fragmentation and hostility characterising the region's international relations. There is little that binds its states and societies together but much that divides them. Any chance of finding unifying common ground against the West has long since disappeared. As the particular distortions imposed by the Cold War unravel, many historical patterns that were either suppressed or overridden by ideological and superpower rivalry are reappearing ... History, therefore, strongly reinforces the view that Asia is in danger of heading back to the future.[4]

Many Asians fear that such passages do not merely contain analytical predictions, but that they also represent Europe's hope that East Asia will not succeed and surpass it.

THE TIDAL WAVE

What is striking about the above articles is a blindness to the biggest tidal wave to hit East Asia, which is the fundamental reason for the region's economic dynamism: the tidal wave of common sense and confidence. Over the past decade or two an immense psychological revolution has occurred and is continuing in most East Asian minds: increasing numbers realise that they have wasted centuries trying to make it into the modern world. They can no longer afford to do so. After centuries, their moment has come. Why waste it over relatively petty disputes or historical squabbles?

It is difficult for a European or North American to understand the momentous nature of this psychological revolution because they cannot step into East Asian minds. Their minds have never been wrapped in the cellophane of colonialism. They have never had to struggle with the subconscious assumption that perhaps they are second-rate human beings, never good enough to be "number one". The growing realisation among East Asians that they can match, if not better, other cultures or societies has led to an explosion of confidence.

This confidence is further bolstered by their awareness that the time needed to catch up with the developed world is getting progressively shorter. The period that nations take to double output per head is shortening—the United Kingdom took 58 years (from 1780), the United States 47 years (from 1839), Japan 33 years (from the 1880s), Indonesia 17 years, South Korea 11 years, China 10 years. The reasons are complex, but they include the faster spread of technology, ideas and business practices, and, of course, the rapid movement of capital across borders.

Many East Asians are also increasingly aware that they are doing some fundamental things correctly in their societies in contrast to many European societies. Many European thinkers celebrate the firm implantation of democracies in their societies as an unmitigated good, especially since it prevents wars. But democratic systems can also be deeply resistant to change. The heavy welfare burdens accumulated by Europe cannot be shed easily, especially since the burden is often passed to future generations. The American Bureau of the Budget recently forecast that for an American infant born this year, the tax requirement to pay for existing programmes will be 82 percent of his lifetime earnings. William Rees-Mogg notes that "this figure is obviously unsupportable", but adds that "government spending in Europe is actually higher than it is in the US".[5]

Several of Europe's socio-economic policies are fundamentally untenable. Since 1977, Europe has created only 9 million jobs compared to 30 million in the United States and Canada. During this period, most of the jobs created in the US were in the private sector, while in Europe they were in the public sector. As a consequence, taxation in Europe is increasing and the social cost linked to wages is, on average, twice that of the United States.[6]

Some forecasts already indicate a 1 percent annual drop in real European disposable income over the next 25 years. A European child born today faces the prospect of earning less than his parents. By contrast, East Asians are aware that they are about to be carried up by a huge rising tide. This year, the total GDP, in real purchasing-power terms, of the 2.5 billion people in China, India, Japan and the Asian rim is probably about half that of the 800 million in Europe and North America. By 2025, the Asian GDP will be double the Euro-American.[7]

Over 100 years ago, Japan was the first Asian society to attempt to enter the modern world, with the Meiji Restoration. What followed, however, were decades of military conflict which, after some initial successes in the Sino-Japanese and the Russo-Japanese wars, led to disaster and ignominy. Is it not conceivable that 100 years later, East Asia could follow the same path: economic modernisation leading eventually to military conflict and disaster?

But there is something crucially different between what Japan tried to do 100 years ago and what East Asia is attempting now. Japan believed fervently that it could become successful only if it joined the premier club of the world then: the club of colonisers. As Richard J. Samuels says, "Japan's early industrialisation was led by military industries to enhance national security by 'catching up and surpassing the West'." This mobilisation was captured by the slogan "Rich Nation, Strong Army" (*fukoku kyohei*).[8] Economic modernisation was not a goal in itself, but was, as shown by Europe in the preceding century or two, a stepping stone to military conquest.

The dynamic in East Asia today could not be more different than the environment Japan experienced in the later 19th century. East Asia is trying to achieve something much more fundamental: it wants to succeed in its own right, without trying to become a member of a European Club. It will be an immense struggle to work out social, political and philosophical norms that best capture their people's aspirations, but it will also be an all-engrossing struggle. The most foolish thing that any East Asian society could do is to turn away from this overwhelming challenge and engage in traditional military rivalries: to snatch failure once more from the jaws of victory.

COMPARING GEO-STRATEGIC ENVIRONMENTS:
EUROPE AND EAST ASIA

Conventional European thinkers are likely to be unmoved by this picture of a great human drama unfolding in East Asia. They focus their strategic sights either on ancient and smouldering rivalries, or on arms races. As indicated above, conventional wisdom suggests that East Asia, in contrast to Europe, is likely to experience a much less benign strategic environment.

Buzan and Segal reinforce this point by looking at the role of what they call "international society" in maintaining international peace and stability. As they say: "International society encompasses the more specific notion of regimes. It suggests a situation in which a whole set of regimes, multilateral organisations and rules exists that enables states to communicate on a regular basis, to establish modes and habits of consultation and cooperation, to coordinate and manage their relations, and to prevent their disputes escalating into conflict of war." They add, "Europe, in particular, and the West, in general, constitute advanced and richly developed international societies. What is distinctive about Asia is its combination of several industrialised societies with a regional international society so impoverished in its development that it compares poorly with even Africa and the Middle East."[9]

Such conventional wisdom, however, fails to acknowledge a fundamental fact in comparing Europe with East Asia: while the guns are quiet in East Asia, Europe is surrounded by a ring of fire, stretching from the tremors in Algeria that ripple through North Africa, surface again in the vicious fighting in Bosnia, and reach a climax in the Caucasus. From the conflict in Georgia to the explosions waiting to burst in Kosovo, Macedonia and Albania, more lives are lost daily on the periphery of Europe than in the entire Asia-Pacific region, which has a much larger population.

In comparing East Asia with Europe, several writers stress that the presence of developed regional institutions, like the North Atlantic Treaty Organisation (NATO), the European Union (EU) and the Organisation on Security and Cooperation in Europe (OSCE), gives Europe a competitive advantage in peace and security. OSCE has even been suggested as a model for the Asia-Pacific region. But of the 53 members of OSCE, the following are experiencing either internal or external conflicts: Serbia, Croatia, Bosnia, Armenia, Azerbaijan, Georgia, Moldova and Tajikistan, not to mention the conflict brewing in Macedonia and Kosovo. The silence of the guns in the Asia-Pacific and the roar of the guns around Europe is not an accident, but is a result of the fact that Europe's approach to its immediate environment is strategically incoherent, while East Asia is making relatively sound strategic decisions.

There are several flawed elements in Europe's strategically incoherent policies. The first is Europe's belief that it could secure peace by concentrating on the internal unification of Europe while detaching itself from its periphery. To an observer from East Asia, all the efforts to deepen unification through the Maastricht Treaty or widen unification by incorporating "similar" European countries into the European Union seem like a household working to rearrange the living room furniture while ignoring the flood waters seeping in from the rising tides just outside the door. It is puzzling that Europe is trying to draw up its ramparts to cut itself off from its neighbours—excluding them from its growth and prosperity and keeping them as outsiders. In contrast, the strategic impulse in East Asia is to draw all societies into the region's dynamism, starting with Myanmar and Vietnam and eventually including North Korea.

Europe has no choice but to deal with three major forces on its doorstep: Russia, Africa and Islam. In a shrinking world, the turbulence in these three areas will seep into Europe. While Europe has had a marginally successful strategy towards Russia (questions remain about its long-term viability), it has had a fundamentally flawed strategy towards Africa and Islam.

From a long-term perspective, it may have been a strategic error for Europe to admit socially and culturally similar states into the EU ahead of Turkey. It sent a signal that Europe would always be cut off from the world of Islam: that no state in the Islamic world, no matter how secular, modernised or "European", would be admitted into the "house of Europe". An opportunity was lost to demonstrate that an Islamic society could cross cultural boundaries and be like any other modern European state. Europe may also have lost a valuable opportunity to demonstrate that it can transcend its cultural boundaries and create, as the Asia-Pacific has done, region-wide institutions, such as the Association of South-East Asian Nations (ASEAN), the Asia-Pacific Economic Cooperation Conference (APEC) and the ASEAN Regional Forum (ARF), which contain a wide variety of cultures.

This exclusion of the Islamic world has been magnified by European passivity in the face of genocide at its doorstep in Bosnia. Few in the Islamic world (or elsewhere) believe that Europe would have been as passive if Muslim artillery shells had been raining down on Christian populations in Sarajevo or Srebrenica. It does not help that Europe condemns the reversal of democracy in Myanmar while endorsing a similar reversal in Algeria. Such double standards are easily shrugged off by cynical Europeans. But they underestimate the enormous price Europe is paying in alienating a force, Islam, that it will have to live with for the next thousand years. For the past few decades, one of Europe's greatest strengths has been its moral leadership: often providing the right moral responses and massive humanitarian assistance to major crises. Gradually European leaders are waking up to the magnitude of the problem. German Chancellor Helmut Kohl asserted this year that "the rise of Islamic fundamentalism in North Africa is the major threat" to Europe, while Prime Minister Edouard Balladur of France has called the fundamentalist revolution in Algeria the leading threat to his country.[10]

A second flawed element in European strategy is the assumption that the rest of the world, including its neighbours, will follow the European social idea—the natural progression of history will lead to all societies becoming liberal-democratic and capitalist. For most Europeans, this assumption was vindicated when Russian President Mikhail Gorbachev followed this path. The Soviet Union's subsequent collapse and disappearance further vindicated it. Hence, it was natural that so many Europeans embraced the idea that "the end of history" had come with the universal applicability of the Western idea.

This profound belief in the superiority of the Western idea creates a unique weakness or blindness for Europe: an inability to accept the simple notion that other cultures or societies may have equal validity. An essay entitled "Islam and the West" in the *Economist* demonstrates this blindness.[11] The article assumes that for Islamic societies to progress, they must become more like the West. Not once does it suggest that the West may have something to learn from Islam. Again, to suggest a simple contrast, both the world's most populous Islamic state (Indonesia) and the world's most economically successful Islamic state (Malaysia) are in the Asia-Pacific. There is no suggestion in the region that they should follow some other model. This belief in the universality of the Western idea can block the acceptance of the principle of diversity and prevent a region living in peace with other cultures. The Asia-Pacific is used to diversity, but Europe is not.

A third flawed element in European strategy is its effort to "lock in" the relatively high living standards of Europe by raising new barriers to free trade and sustaining high subsidies. Here, the contrast between the strategies of the United States and Europe is striking. The United States has taken the relatively bold leap of crossing a cultural as well as a socio-economic divide by entering into a free-trade agreement with Mexico. Effectively it had no choice because if it did not export some low-paying jobs to Mexico and gain high-paying jobs in return (in a "win-win" arrangement), Mexico could not and would not stop exporting its populace into the United States.

The only permanent solution to the inevitable long-term problem of illegal immigration into Europe is to export some low-paying jobs (in return for high-paying jobs) and enter into free-trade agreements, initially with North Africa. In the long run this strategy is more likely to work if Europe promotes (rather than hinders) global free-trade regimes that will integrate Europe and its neighbours into the rising tide of prosperity in the Asia-Pacific. But to allow Europe's neighbours to compete in their areas of natural comparative advantage, European agricultural subsidies have to be abolished. It is quite frightening that such a simple, sensible solution to Europe's long-term strategic problem is considered virtually inconceivable.

In 1990, the ratio of Europe's population to Africa's was 498 million to 642 million; according to United Nations projections, by 2050, based on medium fertility extension, the ratio will be 486 million to 2.27 billion—a ratio akin to the white-black ratio in today's South

Africa. Within a few decades, Western Europe will be confronted with impoverished masses on its borders, and increasing numbers will be slipping in to join the millions already there.[12] Unless these masses feel that they are a part of European prosperity in their homeland, they will feel no choice but to move into the "house of Europe".

Some writers are beginning to recognise that Africa is Europe's problem. William Pfaff recently asked, "Who is responsible for the African catastrophe?" and answered, "The European powers, who colonised Africa in the nineteenth century out of an immensely complex mixture of good and bad motives, thereby destroying Africa's existing social and political systems, its customary institutions and law." He then asked, "Who outside Africa has an urgent material interest in Africa's salvation?" and his answer was, "The Europeans. Besides the fact that Europe is the principal consumer of African mineral and agricultural exports, Africa's foundering means that hundreds of thousands, even millions more desperate people are attempting to get out of Africa to places where they can find order, jobs, security, a future. Their scarcely controllable migration towards Europe already has created immense social problems and serious political tensions."[13]

These flawed elements in European strategy mean a similar impulse is being exported to the rest of the world. I call this the "Atlantic impulse": moving towards continental unification rather than global integration; and exporting political development ahead of economic development while ignoring social and cultural differences and creating new protectionist barriers to "lock in" untenable welfare-state policies. If Europe persists with the Atlantic impulse, it will be a loss not only for Europe, but also for the rest of the world, which has benefited so much from European creativity and dynamism.

A CONCRETE EXAMPLE OF THE ATLANTIC IMPULSE
The Uruguay Round (UR) of the General Agreement on Tariffs and Trade (GATT) negotiations, which was deadlocked from 1989 to 1993

because of European intransigence, illustrates how the Atlantic impulse can damage global interests. It would have probably ended in disaster if not for the crucial APEC leaders meeting in Seattle in November 1993. The United States cleverly sent a signal that if the UR broke down, it would have no choice but to create an Asia-Pacific free-trade area or regime. The other APEC leaders supported this message, and, after a few critical phone calls between Bonn and Paris, Europe finally decided to sign the UR agreements in December 1993.

It was then decided that the final signing ceremony would be held in Marrakesh, Morocco. Unfortunately, the location of this close to the Atlantic led to the surfacing of the Atlantic impulse through an event that almost undermined the final agreement. After gaining the APEC countries' support to secure European approval of the UR agreement, the United States suddenly switched sides and teamed up with Europe to try to incorporate the "social clause" into the agreement. The social clause is ostensibly designed to improve working conditions in the Third World. Many Europeans defend it as representing a moral impulse. In doing so, they insult the intelligence of the rest of the world, who find it hard to accept that the Europeans are morally interested in the fate of these workers now that their incomes are rising but were not interested when their incomes were stagnant. The social clause is a charade that will not be of any benefit to Europe.

Working with the Europeans caused the United States to suffer because it was poorly received by its APEC partners, a point that some gracious US officials admit in private. But this whole episode had even greater significance. It demonstrated that the US, given its geographical location, will be torn between the Atlantic and the Pacific impulses over the decades to come. Over the next 10 years, American choices will probably be the most pivotal factor in international relations.

THE UNITED STATES: ATLANTIC OR PACIFIC FIRST?

During the Cold War, the geopolitical environment for the United States was clear. The threat came from the Soviet Union, and the

Atlantic alliance was the most important security priority. When victory came, the then secretary of state, James Baker, captured the sweetness of the moment by declaring the creation of a community stretching from Vancouver to Vladivostok (a circle that virtually covered the whole world except the intervening Pacific Ocean). It was probably the finest moment for the Atlantic impulse.

The interests that will link the United States across the Atlantic and Pacific Oceans to Europe and East Asia, respectively, will increasingly diverge. Culturally, the United States will look to Europe for its roots. The political and military institutions will also remain stronger across the Atlantic: institutions as varied as the Group of Seven (G-7), the OSCE, NATO and the Organisation for Economic Cooperation and Development (OECD) will attract American leaders across the Atlantic. These links will endure.

But the economic and, perhaps, overall national security of the United States will be determined increasingly by developments across the Pacific. Last year, trans-Pacific trade totalled $330 billion—50 percent greater than trans-Atlantic trade. The ratio will reach 2 to 1 by the end of this decade.

There is no doubt which the future growth markets are. By incorporating four more states into the European Union in January 1995, the EU will add 29 million consumers. Even if the larger Eastern European states (Czech Republic, Slovakia, Hungary and Poland) are included, there will be an increase of 65 million consumers. In contrast, in East Asia alone there are 1,840 million consumers, and, as greater numbers of them reach the critical benchmark of $1,000 per capita per year, their demand for consumer products grows. Immediately beyond East Asia, India has a soaring middle class (200 million now and 400 million within a decade) and upper class (40 million).

The eyes of strategic thinkers glaze over when consumer products are discussed rather than nuclear proliferation. But major strategic decisions are influenced by consumer markets. In June 1994, the United States finally lifted a major cloud hanging over the Asia-Pacific region by de-linking China's Most Favoured Nation (MFN) status from non-trade issues. The critical factor in this decision was the potential size of China's consumer market. (It appears to have been the strong and determined leadership of the United States that defused the North Korean nuclear crisis. Future historians will record that ultimately even leaders like Kim Il Sung and Kim Jong Il were conditioned by regional dynamics not to behave like Saddam Hussein.)

But economics alone will not draw the United States closer to the Pacific. The larger socio-political and military-security environments, as well as cultural comfort, are equally crucial factors. There is a deeply held belief among European strategic thinkers, as well as among the Atlanticists who live close to the Atlantic shores of the United States, that the United States will trade across the Pacific, but be a member of the Atlantic community. Indeed, even the idea of a Pacific community is dismissed because of the diversity and cleavages in the region.

It may therefore be useful to discuss what a possible Pacific community would look like, and how it would differ from the Atlantic community. It will come as a surprise to many Europeans to learn that a vision of such a community is already emerging and, more importantly, that some of the initial foundations have already been laid. And this, in turn, explains why the Pacific impulse is increasing in the United States day by day.

THE PACIFIC COMMUNITY: A VISION
There has never been anything like a Pacific community before. Hence, those who try to discern the future of the Pacific from its past will be blind to its possibilities. It will be unlike anything that existed before because it will be neither an Asian community nor an American community. The Pacific has the potential to become the most dynamic region in the world because it can bring together the best from several streams of rich civilisations in Asia and the West and, if the fusion works, the creativity could be on a scale never seen or experienced before.

There has already been some such creativity. The dynamism of East Asia is not purely a renaissance of rich ancient cultures: it is the result of a successful fusion of East and West in the reconstruction of their societies. Japan has already demonstrated what success such a formula can bring. Culturally, it remains quintessentially Japanese, but its civil administration (with arguably the most powerful "Westernised" rational bureaucracy in the world), business, science and technology are among the best in the world. It has modernised and is no longer a feudal society (several key imperial ceremonies are conducted in coat tails and Japan has one of the most Europeanised courts in the world), but the Japanese remain Japanese. While many Japanese teenagers look superficially like their European or American counterparts, their homes are Japanese, their souls are Japanese and they are reverential towards their elders. And there is relatively little juvenile delinquency or crime. The deep glue that holds Asian societies and families together has not been eroded by modernisation.

The result, in the eyes of many, is an economic and industrial miracle. Japanese productivity in most manufacturing sectors cannot be matched by any other work force in the world. But this success is due neither to Japanese culture nor to Western methods: it is a result of the combination of the two.

This is why the efforts of American trade negotiators to create a "level playing field" by juggling with trade rules and regimes is seen by many in Asia to be a futile exercise. On a totally level playing field, most Japanese industries will outperform their American counterparts (even though there will be many areas in which the United States will continue to excel). Kenneth Courtis pointed out in an address to the Pacific Basin Economic Council of Canada on 18 April 1994: "For example, in 1993, in its third year of the most difficult recession of the past four decades, Japan committed 18.2% of its GNP to capital investment. In contrast, the figure was only 12% of GNP for the United States. At the peak of an investment-led GNP expansion last year Japan invested some $5,777 per capita in new plants and equipment, while

America invested $2,519 per capita." In the long run, the United States will be able to match Japan when it undergoes a parallel process of osmosis: absorbing the best of Asian civilisations as East Asia has been absorbing the best of the West.

The real success of the Pacific community will come when the learning process in the region becomes a two-way, rather than a one-way, street. It took a long time for China and other East Asian societies to accept the sensible advice of Yukichi Fukuzawa, the Meiji reformer, "to progress and learn from the West". An American, William Smith Clark, is worshipped in Sapporo because he inspired young Japanese with his remark "Boys, be ambitious". When an American town proclaims a Japanese (or any other East Asian) as a hero will mark the arrival of a two-way street of ideas.

Some progress, however, has been made. Japanese quality-control methods (which were conceived by an American, Arthur Demming) have begun to be transplanted to America. The American car industry is finally eager to learn from Japan, and the United States is now keen to study Japanese methods in specific industrial fields.

Real learning requires humility. Fortunately, the Americans are fundamentally an open and compassionate people. They carry no hubris from history, as the Europeans do. Only this can explain why the United States has been the most benevolent great power in history. European nations with such power would have used it to advance only their own national interests. Americans pushed an idea. And they have contributed to uplifting East Asian society. East Asia would not be where it is today if it had not been for the generosity of the Sterling Fashion American spirit. With each passing day, the bright young East Asian minds driving the economic effervescence of the region increasingly come from American universities. The United States provides the bridges for the fusion of East and West in the Pacific.

History demonstrates that trade brings with it not just money and goods, but also ideas. The sheer explosion of two-way trade cannot leave the two cultures across the Pacific intact. Over time a fusion will take place. When such fusion is perceived by the American body politic as a positive development in reinvigorating American society, the consensus, for example in favour of a continuing strong US military presence as a stabilising factor, will grow. It is evident that such fusion has already begun, with beneficial effects, especially for regional security.

THE ASIA-PACIFIC: REGIONAL SECURITY

It is not an accident that a region that has experienced some of the greatest wars of the 20th century is now the most peaceful. There must be deeper forces behind this. Some have been touched on earlier in this article. Others may be hard to substantiate, but they deserve consideration. For example, one reason could be the decoupling of East Asian security from European concerns. The two "hot wars" fought in East Asia, Korea and Vietnam, were fundamentally "undertaken in large part because of a perceived linkage to European security".[14] Facile explanations also have to be questioned. US military superiority in the region cannot be the only explanation (although it is undoubtedly important). If military superiority is critical, NATO should have prevented the crisis in Bosnia.

The Asia-Pacific region is developing a unique "corporate culture" on regional security: an unusual blend of East and West. It combines both Western concepts (for example, of national sovereignty as well as regional organisation) and Eastern attitudes on managing differences. The best current working model is found in Southeast Asia.

Just like Europe, the continent of Asia has its own Balkans that are also tucked away in its southeast corner. In size and diversity, however, Southeast Asia far exceeds the Balkans. It has over 450 million people, which is 10 times the population of the Balkans. In both ethnic and religious terms, it is far more diverse: Islam, Christianity, Buddhism (two schools), Hinduism, Taoism and Confucianism coexist. And, as recently as 10 years ago, Southeast Asia elicited far greater pessimism than the Balkans. In 1984, the guns had been silent in Europe since

World War II, but Southeast Asia had experienced communist insurgencies and more deaths during the Cold War than anywhere else.

Until as recently as 1965, the prospects for Southeast Asia looked bleak. Indonesia had experienced instability and economic decline under Sukarno; *confrontasi* against Malaysia and Singapore was continuing; Sabah was disputed by the Philippines and Malaysia; Singapore had experienced a problematic and painful merger with Malaysia; and communist insurgencies were rife in the region. All of these countries believed that the tide of history was with them. Hence, the conventional wisdom, less than 30 years ago, was that Southeast Asian states would "fall like dominoes". Thus, Southeast Asia should be wary of excessive optimism.

So how has Southeast Asia become the most successful part of the Third World? It is now experiencing a peace that is the envy of most of the world. And, in what is perhaps the greatest irony, the guns in the Balkans of Asia are quiet while the sound of gunfire in the Balkans of Europe suggests that it is Europe, rather than Asia, that is experiencing a "back to the future".

Southeast Asia has used several elements of the "corporate culture" for regional security. The first is the deeply rooted Asian tradition (symbolically represented by visitors taking off their shoes before entering someone's home) of respecting the household and recognising that one enters as a guest. Hence, virtually every Asian society endorses the principle of non-interference in internal affairs. This is an old adage that also has its roots in Europe. But with the rise of universalistic assumptions in Western societies, this principle has been eroded.

In much of Europe and North America, it is considered "legitimate" to intervene in the internal affairs of a state when certain universal principles are violated, especially human rights. In North America or a Europe exhausted by war, this leads to no conflicts. But, as the experience of South Asia demonstrates, commenting on internal affairs can lead to conflict in less developed states. One essential reason why no war has broken out among ASEAN states for over 25 years is precisely that they adhere to the principle of non-interference in internal affairs.

ASEAN has been heavily criticised for remaining silent on East Timor. If most Asian countries do not comment on each other's domestic activities, it is probably because they believe in the old Christian adage "Let he who has not sinned cast the first stone". All our societies are imperfect, but if we are all progressing towards a better state of affairs, why rock the boat? There is a lot of wisdom in the decision, for example, of Japan to exercise restraint in commenting on China. This supposedly "immoral" stand could in the long run save millions of lives by preventing conflict.

A second element is the Asian way of dealing with difficult relations. Apart from the propaganda crossing the ideological divide between North and South Korea (and to a lesser extent between China and Taiwan), it is striking how few East Asian nations engage in "shouting matches" with each other. "Face" is important, and conflict can break out when it is lost, such as when Vietnam humiliated China by invading Kampuchea in defiance of explicit Chinese warnings. Vietnamese diplomats have confessed in private that it had gone against 2,000 years of collected wisdom in snubbing China so openly.

But Asians also accept hierarchy. When this is not violated, peace can reign. The fascination of Sino-Japanese relations is in deciding who should view who as number one. Economically, Japan is far ahead, but in political and military terms, China carries more weight. Japan is more stable than China in the short term, and China needs Japanese economic aid and investment. But Japan needs China's market, as well as social stability in China. While Japan's culture is derived from China, Japan carries more weight in the international hierarchy. So who determines who is number one? There will be no explicit statements or understandings, but it was significant that the Japanese emperor chose to visit China in 1992, at a time when Beijing was still relatively isolated internationally. This was an unusually generous gesture on the part of Japan and may have bought a decade or two of stability to their relations. Symbolic gestures are important in Asia.

These elements indicate the different dynamics operating in the Atlantic and the Pacific. The Atlantic believes in building strong institutions: NATO, the EU and the OSCE are the strongest in their field. Together they ensure that none of the members are directly threatened by a military invasion. But, in an era when invasions are virtually inconceivable outside the usual "tinderbox" regions (for example, the Middle East, South Asia), these powerful institutions seem powerless either to defend their members from non-traditional sources of insecurity (such as rising immigrants and terrorism), or to prevent nearby conflicts (such as Algeria and Bosnia).

The Pacific has no comparable institutions, but is creating networks instead. These are inclusive rather than exclusive, but, even more unusual (and this goes against the conventional wisdom in many European textbooks on international relations), their formation is driven not by the major powers, but by the middle or small powers (especially ASEAN countries). None of the recent regional initiatives were either conceived or built upon in the major capitals.

The annual July gathering of ASEAN foreign ministers was originally confined to the six member-states. Gradually, others applied to attend: the European Community (1972), Australia (1974), New Zealand (1975), Japan (1977), Canada (1977), the United States (1977) and Korea (1991). There were no heavy agendas, formal communiqués or attempts to create Helsinki-type "baskets". Instead, ASEAN emphasised personal contacts and trust-building.

These July meetings paved the way for the creation of two larger region-wide institutions: APEC and the ARF. When APEC was first suggested by Australia, the United States demurred. When the rest of the region agreed to proceed without it, Washington decided to join. Initially, the United States was an unenthusiastic participant, but when Malaysia suggested establishing an East Asian Economic Caucus (EAEC), Washington decided that the best way to fight the EAEC was to strengthen APEC. Hence, the United States offered to host the first APEC leaders meeting in Seattle in November 1993—surely the most powerful gathering of leaders in the world (if judged by the portion of the world's GNP and population represented at the meeting). Now these APEC leaders meetings are becoming an annual event and, virtually out of nowhere, a powerful institution has been established. Its quick and sure-footed arrival only makes sense when viewed against the larger dynamic working in the region.

The ARF was launched in Bangkok in July 1994. Japan originally suggested it, but nothing came of it. It did become a reality, however, when ASEAN adopted the idea. After attending several ASEAN meetings, the major powers had confidence in ASEAN's ability to be an impartial but effective leader of the process. Viewed from the inside, the process seems chaotic. But viewed from the outside, it seems amazing how quickly and firmly the ARF has been established. There will eventually be an ARF summit.

APEC and the ARF are unique because the culture that guides both institutions is a blend of East and West. The rules of procedure are Western; English is the only language spoken at meetings of officials; golf, a game with Scottish origins, is the one game they all play; but the behavioural culture within the organisation is heavily influenced by Asia. Direct confrontation is avoided—"face" must not be lost. Everybody must feel "comfortable". And in both cases diversity makes them stronger. The presence of culturally diverse but comfortable "pairs" like Australia and Indonesia, Canada and Korea, Japan and Thailand, the US and ASEAN, and China and Malaysia, to name a few, gives the Asia-Pacific region its uniqueness.

Both APEC and the ARF, of course, are fragile new institutions. If they collapse within a year or two, or even within a decade, many assumptions about the future course of the Asia-Pacific will have been proved wrong. I have to submit my thesis to such empirical verification.

But there is good reason for confidence. APEC can only move as fast as its chairman can drive it. It has no EU-type bureaucracy to carry it. Under the leadership of US President Bill Clinton, it was not surprising that the Seattle meeting succeeded. The chairmanship, however, could not have been passed to a more different actor: Indonesian President Suharto, a quintessential Javanese leader. Yet the Bogor Meeting that he chaired proved even more successful than the Seattle meeting, especially in setting a definite timetable for moving towards freer trade in the Asia-Pacific region.

The next APEC summit will be in Japan, which has already expressed reservations about the rapid pace of trade liberalisation with APEC. Some feel that Japanese bureaucrats will be inclined to slow down the progress of APEC. But Japanese leaders and thinkers are also aware that the results of the summit in Japan will be measured against the two preceding summits in the United States and Indonesia and the two succeeding summits in the Philippines and Canada. If Japan's contribution to APEC suffers in such comparison, Japan's claim to international leadership would also have been dented. As the date for the Osaka summit in November 1995 approaches, Japan will be under pressure to deliver results.

If APEC can be safely passed from one end of the cultural spectrum of the Asia-Pacific to the other without any mishap, it suggests that institutions like APEC and the ARF are riding on a larger, more powerful underlying dynamic, which is what I call the "Pacific impulse".

Neither the Pacific nor the Atlantic impulse, however, is geographically bound. There is no reason why Europe cannot link itself closely to East Asia, as North America is doing. The recent decision by the European Union to launch an "Asia Policy" was a welcome move. If both North America and Europe were to develop the Pacific impulse, we may actually enjoy 50 more years not just of relative peace across most parts of the globe, but also a rising tide of prosperity. The opportunities are enormous.

1. Kenneth S. Courtis, "The Centre of the World Economy Shifts to the Asia-Pacific: Challenges and Opportunities for Canada", an address to the Pacific Basin Economic Council of Canada, Toronto, 18 April 1994.

2. Richard K. Betts, "Wealth, Power and Instability", *International Security*, vol. 18, no. 3, Winter 1993–94, p. 64.

3. Aaron L. Friedberg, "Ripe for Rivalry", *International Security*, vol. 18, no. 3, Winter 1993–94, p. 7.

4. Barry Buzan and Gerald Segal, "Rethinking East Asian Security", *Survival*, vol. 36, no. 2, Summer 1994, p. 7.

5. William Rees-Mogg, "Money Moves East, as Welfare goes West", *The Straits Times* (Singapore), 9 July 1994, p. 35.

6. Stephanie Gazelline, "World Competitiveness Today: New Rules for a New Era", *European Business Report*, Spring 1994, p. 22.

7. Rees-Mogg, op. cit.

8. Richard J. Samuels, *Rich Nation, Strong Army: National Security and the Technological Transformation of Japan*, Cornell University Press, 1994.

9. Buzan and Segal, op. cit.

10. Daniel Pipes, "Why the Stakes Are so High in Algeria", *International Herald Tribune*, 13 August 1994.

11. "Islam and the West", *The Economist*, 6–12 August 1994.

12. Kishore Mahbubani, "The West and the Rest", *The National Interest*, no. 28, Summer 1992, pp. 5–6.

13. William Pfaff, "Africa Needs Europe to Get Involved Again in a Different Spirit", *International Herald Tribune*, 15 August 1994, p. 4.

14. Betts, op. cit.

AN ASIA-PACIFIC CONSENSUS

FOREIGN AFFAIRS, SEPTEMBER/OCTOBER 1997.

In the autumn of 1997 *Foreign Affairs* decided to produce a special commemorative 75th anniversary volume. I felt honoured to be chosen as one of the writers to contribute, especially since I was the only voice from East Asia. The editors said that I could write on any topic. I could think of only one appropriate subject for *Foreign Affairs* readers: to alert them that in the world to come the Asia-Pacific would naturally provide the main locus of world history for the 21st century. Most strategic thinkers had begun to hint that the emergence of new powers on the world stage, especially China, would lead to conflict and turbulence. Joseph Nye was right in reminding us that this has been the natural course of world history since the days of the Greeks. In my essay, I tried to point out that the Asia-Pacific could try to avoid this natural groove of history by forging a new consensus, an Asia-Pacific consensus.

HISTORY'S NEW HINGE

Since the 19th century, the world economy's centre of gravity has shifted steadily westward from Europe to North America and now to the Asia-Pacific. As the economic centre shifts, the new locus becomes the main theatre of global action. From the two World Wars to the Cold War, the course of the 20th century was determined primarily in Europe. In the 21st century, the Asia-Pacific will become this hinge of history.

As this century nears its end, it is distressing to see how few minds have focused on what needs to be done to keep the region on track. The constant attention to individual issues—Korea, Taiwan, Hong Kong, the Spratly Islands—ignores the dynamics of the bigger picture. In the past decade, the region has taken several big strides forward in terms of economic growth and political tranquillity, with only occasional steps backward, like the Taiwan Strait crisis last year. The Asia-Pacific can still take more steps forward, but only if the key players reach a new consensus on the region's future.

This consensus could rest on three distinct and somewhat unusual pillars. First, the current geopolitical order should be frozen in place. Under present circumstances no better order can be achieved. Second, all key players must develop a common understanding of the region's constraints and realities. Third, they will need a vision that draws out common elements from the region's tremendous diversity and so lay the groundwork for a sense of community.

It is easy to understand how Europe is being brought together by legal compact or how the Atlantic is united by a sense of community. But the Asia-Pacific, being more diverse, requires more consensus-building. The main reason Southeast Asia—the Balkans of Asia—has held together is such consensus-building.

As the single strongest power on the eve of the 21st century, the United States will play a pivotal role. The United States has a window of opportunity to move the Asia-Pacific, and consequently world history, down the right path. But for it to do so alone would deplete the deep reservoir of goodwill it has accumulated in the region and damage its long-term national interests. During the Cold War, the collective economic growth, military strength and population of the NATO countries far exceeded those of the Warsaw Pact. But the 260 million people of the United States cannot nudge the 1.8 billion people of East Asia on their own. This will have to be a team effort.

IF IT AIN'T BROKE …

The economic resurgence in East Asia will shift the relative power of the leading players. China is the big question. In the first half of the 21st century, China's economy will almost certainly grow larger than that of the United States. When that happens, the world's established power structure will have to adjust to China's arrival; Washington may no longer be the modern Rome. Some minds there have begun flirting with the idea of containment. Though rarely discussed openly, there is a tendency to believe that since it worked against the Soviet Union, it could work against another communist giant.

But containment is a nonstarter. US-led and unilateral sanctions against Iraq, Cuba and China have failed to topple regimes or to change their behaviour significantly. The United States will probably stand alone if it decides to contain China. The major European states declined to support the 1997 Human Rights Resolution against China in Geneva, nor did they join the American and British boycott of the swearing-in of Hong Kong's new legislature. China poses no direct threat to Europe. On the contrary, the vast and rapidly growing Chinese and East Asian economies offer immense opportunities for rejuvenating Europe. Europe is realistic, and it will engage China as a partner.

The 500 million people of Southeast Asia, soon to be united by the expansion of the Association of Southeast Asian Nations (ASEAN), will also serve to check containment. The current generation of Southeast Asian leaders still remember China's behaviour during Mao's heyday, when Beijing supported communist insurgencies against them. But China's rulers now seem to be moving the Middle Kingdom in the same direction as ASEAN states, concentrating on economic development and burying political differences, to the benefit of all.

... DON'T FIX IT

Rejection of containment does not mean acceptance of appeasement. If China's rise is causing disquiet among policymakers in Washington, it is similarly unsettling other capitals, from Tokyo to Moscow, from New Delhi to Canberra.

China should understand why there is a strong impulse in the region to retain elements of the status quo. The US military presence is one key element. There is a consensus in Washington's defence establishment that this presence should not be scaled back. But officials must convince Congress and the American public why this should be so, especially when there is no clear military threat to American interests. The challenge will become even more acute after Korea's reunification, which may happen sooner rather than later.

American interests in the Asia-Pacific region have grown to an extent that is not fully appreciated. In 1996, the United States' overall trade with Asia stood at $570 billion, compared to $270 billion with Europe. Trade matters more and more to the United States. Exports today make up 30 percent of the United States' GDP, up from 13 percent in 1970 and 25 percent in 1992. While headlines often focus on trade deficits with Asia, few Americans are aware that between 1992 and 1996 the value of American exports to Japan grew 47 percent and exports to the rest of East Asia, excluding China, by the same figure. The United States exports more to Singapore than it does to France or Italy, two partners in the Group of Seven. Altogether 11.5 million high-paying American jobs rely on exports to the world. Trade flows are matched by increasing investment and tourist flows that have created a bubbling cauldron of economic growth on both sides of the Pacific.

Any exodus of US forces from the Asia-Pacific would damage this spectacular economic performance. The region's economic dynamism rests on a stable geopolitical environment, marked by a general absence of conflict or military tension. While there are flash points—Korea, the Senkakuffi Diaoyu Islands, Taiwan, the Spratly Islands—the prevailing balance of power, though delicate, prevents them from igniting. The US military presence buys time—for both the region and the United States.

Officially, China frowns on the US military presence, especially after the dispatch of two aircraft carriers at the height of the Taiwan Strait crisis in March 1996 and the interim review of the US-Japan defence guidelines in June 1997. But Chinese strategists know the alternatives could be worse. Any breakup of the US-Japan military alliance, at a time when Japan feels insecure about China's rise, would leave Japan with no option but to go nuclear.

Washington must be sensitive to Sino-Japanese relations. It was only 100 years ago that the Japanese navy sank the Qing dynasty's fleet, forcing the cession of Taiwan to Japan. China will not easily forget its defeat, humiliation and suffering during this century's Japanese occupation. It will never accept Taiwan falling under the umbrella of the US-Japanese alliance. Although the international media portray Japan as pacifist and China as belligerent, the emotions in both countries are triggered by memories of a different era, when the roles were reversed. China must realise that Japan today is developing equally strong fears and suspicions of it. Never before have China and Japan both been powerful at the same time. It will take a while before open and direct dialogue develops between Beijing and Tokyo. This is one reason the United States is still needed.

ASEAN and Australia have also tried to provide opportunities for Japan and China to meet. Australia initiated the Asia-Pacific Economic Cooperation Forum, which was elevated to the level of heads of state by President Bill Clinton in 1993, providing the only opportunity for the leaders of the United States, Japan and China to come together in the same room. ASEAN also initiated the ASEAN Regional Forum (ARF), the only regional security forum that includes all the major powers. No other regional security forum enjoys both

US and Chinese confidence. Foreign ministers presently meet at the ARF, but the time for an ARF summit of world leaders may have arrived. While APEC is unable to discuss security issues because of Taiwan and Hong Kong's presence, the ARF suffers from no such limitations. In December, another historic meeting will take place when the leaders of China, Japan and South Korea meet with ASEAN leaders in Kuala Lumpur, in the first-ever East Asian summit. With each meeting, distrust is chipped away.

One of the secrets of the region is that the present order serves everyone well. The status quo enables the United States to retain its dominant position, protects Japan and removes the pressure for it to consider unilateral options, and gives China what it really desires: decades of peace in which to achieve modernisation. Although no Chinese leader can forsake the national dream of reunifying with Macau and Taiwan, China has far too many domestic preoccupations to contemplate external adventures. To avoid provoking China's ire, the US-Japanese alliance should remain defensive, should not include Taiwan, and should not be extended or changed without careful consideration of regional concerns. Equally important, the United States and Japan must continue to adhere, in form and spirit, to the one-China policy they declare to be official policy. As long as the world, especially the United States and Japan, respects the one-China policy, China will not make waves.

PACIFIC PARTNERS

As the region navigates its way into the next century, policymakers must recognise the realities and constraints in the Asia-Pacific, the second pillar of the plan for the area's continued progress.

The region must accept and adapt to how policy is made in Washington. It is not made on the basis of wise, carefully considered choices but is, rather, the product of public debate, private consultations, and much disarray. Long-term interests are overridden by the short-term interests of managing the media agenda. Long-overdue bilateral visits, such as between the leaders of the United States and China, are hostage to scandals, confirmed or unconfirmed. A wounded presidency, more the rule than the exception since Lyndon Johnson, further complicates matters. And it is on this axis that world history turns.

For a start, East Asian policymakers must accept that the days of the 1950s and 1960s, when American wealth seemed endless and Uncle Sam reached out generously to the Third World, are over. The only way to anchor the United States in a positive relationship with the region is to demonstrate how much it benefits from its friends in the East. Japanese officials seem unable to understand the contradiction between their economic policies (which alienate Americans, fairly or unfairly) and their security policies (which welcome Americans). These contradictions need to be resolved.

But the United States, in turn, must accept that it cannot turn back the clock of history. The United States cannot turn off the economic explosions it helped begin in East Asia. Indeed, like a chain reaction, the dynamism will continue in Asia until most East Asian countries approach the standard of living of industrialised countries. And economic growth has ignited cultural confidence in East Asian minds. The Asian renaissance is here to stay, with or without American involvement.

No government in the region will swallow a suicide pill, no matter how sugar-coated. For the most part, US human rights policies are the result of a benign impulse to improve the lot of the rest of mankind. But their selective application suggests they are based at least partially on realpolitik rather than universal moral considerations. Although the governments of China and Vietnam distrust each other, they have a united response to US efforts to pry open the government they have in place. They do not see the choice as Americans see it—between dark repression and enlightenment. Rather, they regard the alternatives as the chaos of the past and a future anarchy, resembling the former Soviet Union, if change is too hasty.

The region must also accept that the march of technology is irreversible. The Internet, fax machines and satellite TV have opened up every society in the Asia-Pacific, with the exception of North Korea. The East Asian middle class, whose numbers will soon approach 500 million, is developing an understanding of US society's strengths and weaknesses. Its members can make informed choices about the kind of society they want to create for themselves.

With expanding trade, investment, telecommunications, tele-media and travel flows, the Pacific Ocean is shrinking to a pond. Interdependence will steadily increase. Initially, East Asians will need US markets, investment and technology to grow. But as their markets expand, the dependence will be mutual. Competition among Japanese, European and US multinational companies will be decided by who wins the fastest-growing markets in East Asia. If Caterpillar loses the Chinese market to Komatsu, it will lose more than just one market; it will lose the stream of sales needed to upgrade its technology and competitiveness. Performance in the East Asian marketplace will make or break the next generation of multinational corporations.

This interdependence is perhaps the most important reality for key players to acknowledge. The United States can create turmoil in the region with a sudden military withdrawal. Japan can cause chaos by halting the purchase of US Treasury bills, as Prime Minister Ryutaro Hashimoto recently mentioned publicly. China can raise fears by turning inwards. ASEAN can shift the geopolitical balance by leaning to one side or another. With interdependence, a common understanding of realities and constraints becomes essential.

MORE ALIKE THAN YOU KNOW
Leaders must forge a shared vision that will pull the two sides of the Pacific together. Given the divisive debates of recent years, especially between the United States and Asian countries over democracy and human rights, finding common elements that would appeal to the idealism and interests on both sides of the Pacific may seem impossible.

The Asia-Pacific will take some time to realise the sense of community that has been established across the Atlantic. But a failure to do so may lead the region to drift apart.

The Asia-Pacific faces the danger of a split down the middle of the Pacific Ocean, creating an East-West divide. Theoretically, the odds are in favour of this outcome. But those who live and travel in the region realise that a new order is emerging. While governments and newspapers highlight differences, the quality of people-to-people relationships is bridging the cultural gaps, even between the United States and China. Tens of thousands of Chinese students have returned to China after studying in America, and it is these thousands who are moving up the political ladder, assuming key posts as mayors and vice ministers.

When this generation of Asia-Pacific residents gathers, whether they are American and Chinese, Australian and Indonesian, Japanese and Thai, there is little discomfort or distance. They do business with each other with ease. It is not uncommon for a Hong Kong developer to build a shopping centre in Jakarta, with the architectural design done in Vancouver. Or for a Singapore shipping line to shift its accounts department to Manila while acquiring a second shipping line in California. These growing interactions lead to conversations among people from all corners of the Asia-Pacific, in which they speak readily of the strengths and weaknesses of their respective societies.

One might expect these conversations to be peppered with arguments over democracy and dictatorship. Instead, people compare notes on the problems they have with their own governments and societies, and it turns out that all share a desire for good governance. If the region's goal were good governance rather than one form of government, this shared ideal could be a key element for building a political consensus in the Asia-Pacific. After all, no society has yet achieved a monopoly on good governance.

If measures like political stability, economic growth, poverty alleviation and increasing life expectancy and educational levels were the standard, most Asia-Pacific governments would score well. Impartial reports, like those from the World Bank and the World Economic Forum, can serve as the basis for objective evaluation of governance. One of the most hopeful signs is how closely governments in the region watch their ranking on world competitiveness tables. They recognise that closed societies cannot compete well; nor can those engaged in civil war and conflict. ASEAN's decision not to accept co-Prime Minister Hun Sen's seizure of power by force in Cambodia in July showed that minimum standards of good governance are being established.

Private conversations also reveal a common aspiration to live in a society marked by the rule of law. Most people in the Asia-Pacific welcome the principle of equality under the law, which is the foundation of Western societies. East Asians worry about arbitrary justice, still prevalent in many parts of the region. Indeed, for many East Asian societies with lingering feudal traditions, the introduction of the rule of law could have revolutionary implications.

China's decision to work towards a modern legal system with due process, an independent judiciary, and a modern penal and civil code is a remarkable development. It represents a major departure from both Confucianist thinking and Maoist ideology. If North Americans and East Asians felt the same comfort in the rule of law as they moved from city to city, that could prove one of the strongest bonds for the region.

The extension of domestic law could be matched by an equal acceptance of international law. The Asia-Pacific will take some time to achieve the stability of North America or Western Europe. Unresolved differences like those in the South China Sea are volatile. But the region can learn from ASEAN, which, despite the ethnic, religious, linguistic and political diversity in Southeast Asia, has kept peace among its members for decades.

Another strong strain in the region is the shared objective of economic liberalisation. ASEAN has announced the goal of an ASEAN free-trade area by 2003. In the very first year of implementation, 1993, trade among ASEAN members grew 40 percent. APEC has set goals of 2010 and 2020 for free trade among developed and developing members, respectively. US Trade Representative Charlene Barshefsky has mentioned the possibility of exploring free-trade areas not just up and down the Americas but even across the Pacific, beginning with Australia, New Zealand and Singapore. It is clear that free-trade agreements are the way of the future. The challenge is to strengthen and extend the web.

Shifts in power are usually accompanied by conflict, not consensus. But the Asia-Pacific region can learn from history. The Treaty of Versailles after World War I failed because it tried to block an emerging power, Germany. The same mistake need not be made with China. New powers must be accommodated, not contained. Adjustments must be made. In this day and age, when the ideas of the Enlightenment have spread to all corners of the globe, the adjustments need not take place on battlefields. The world can move to a new order in which societies can compete in social, economic and intellectual fields, and in which those best able to harness the strengths of their entire populations are most likely to triumph. If the Asia-Pacific is to defy the historical odds and make a smooth transition from one order to another, a new consensus must be forged soon.

SEVEN PARADOXES ON ASIA-PACIFIC SECURITY

TEXT OF SPEECH AT EUROPE ASIA FORUM IN SINGAPORE. 21 FEBRUARY 1998.

When the centre of gravity of the world's economy shifts to the Asia-Pacific in the 21st century, this will be accompanied by equally significant geopolitical shifts. The three major powers of the region (and perhaps also the world) will be the United States, China and Japan. How they interact will determine the future of the region as well as affect the rest of the world. A paradoxical Arab proverb warns of the dangers of making predictions: "He who speaks about the future lies even when he tells the truth." This paradox inspired me to make an effort to look at likely outcomes in the Asia-Pacific from a different perspective. I tried to see whether thinking in paradoxes might give us a better glimpse of the future of the Asia-Pacific than straight-line projections. I came up with seven paradoxes when I was asked to address the Europe Asia Forum in February 1998.

We are living in times of great change, of a scale that has probably never before been seen in the history of man. For the first time, the Pacific Ocean will become the centre of world history (just like the Atlantic or the Mediterranean were in the 19th and 20th centuries). The three largest economies in the world in the 21st century will be the United States, China and Japan. Therefore, how these three powers interact will inevitably determine the course of this region's and possibly even the world's history, although I say this with some trepidation in a room full of Europeans.

This triangular relationship will be rich and complex. It will be difficult to capture in linear statements. Hence, I have decided to present seven paradoxes, in the hope that they will bring out the complexity and lead us to be less surprised in the coming months and years.

PARADOX 1

The first paradox, during this period of change, is to preserve the status quo in the Asia-Pacific. What we have today may be a freak of history. We see the emergence of a new great power (China) but with no immediate hint of conflict. The region today is not preparing for war. It is preparing for prosperity—that is the mood and tone of the region. The economic difficulties have only further reinforced the point that economic, not political, issues hold centre stage for now.

The value of status quo was shown when we had a crisis in March 1996. In reaction to perceived efforts by Taiwan to flirt with the idea of independence, China conducted missile tests in the Taiwan Strait. The United States responded with a despatch of aircraft carriers. There was tension in the air.

But this crisis may have been good for the region. The Chinese word for "crisis" is a combination of two characters: "danger" and "opportunity". We faced a danger then, but we also saw a new opportunity because it woke up key minds in Washington, DC, Tokyo and Beijing on the importance of preserving the status quo. A new consensus emerged in the region: "Let sleeping dogs lie." This is why we have not had any major geopolitical crisis in East Asia since March 1996, despite phenomenal historical change in our region.

PARADOX 2

The second paradox is that China has a strong vested interest in the two other powers staying together in an alliance. Last year China was very critical of the US-Japan defence alliance, especially of the possibility of its extension to Taiwan. Quite a campaign was launched against this alliance. Certainly the extension of the US-Japan defence alliance to cover Taiwan would be unacceptable to China. The reason is history. Logically, therefore, it would appear that China would be better off with a break-up of the US-Japan alliance because it would not mean a two-against-one situation.

Paradoxically, however, it is in China's real interest to see the US-Japan defence alliance continue because if it breaks up—and Japan has to defend itself alone—Japan must surely contemplate a nuclear option. It serves neither the interest of China (nor even the United States) to push Japan into that nuclear corner. Hence, China should see in its interest the continuation of the alliance—even though with the end of the Cold War, the focus of alliance cannot be the Soviet Union and it could become an alliance to defend Japan against China.

PARADOX 3

The continuation of the US-Japan defence alliance does not mean that the United States will always remain closer to Japan than to China. The third paradox is that despite common political systems—both are liberal democracies—and common economic systems, as well as a long history of engagement, we should not be surprised if the cultural comfort is greater between China and the United States than between Japan and the United States.

Having said that, let me hasten to add that this is a controversial point. It seems rather bold to suggest that an ostensibly communist society like China could develop greater cultural comfort with an open society like the United States than Japan could. But having observed Chinese and Japanese students in the United States, my sense is that Chinese students integrate better into US culture than Japanese students do. One of Japan's real strengths is its social cohesion (it is possibly the most socially cohesive society in the world) and its cultural uniqueness. The unique Japanese tribe is an asset to mankind.

China, relatively speaking, is a somewhat more open society than Japan. Indeed, in one of its most glorious eras—during the Tang dynasty—it was open and cosmopolitan. If, in the 21st century, China, as it becomes more prosperous, emulates the Tang dynasty, we can see the return of a cosmopolitan society. Hence, you could have a paradoxical situation with the United States and Japan having a defence treaty alliance but, culturally, China and the United States becoming closer.

PARADOX 4

The fourth paradox is that while in the US-Japan-China alliance we have two Asian societies (Japan and China) and one Western society, each of the two Asian societies feels more comfortable relating to the Western country—the United States—than to each other.

Historically, Japan and China have lived together for millennia, 1,000 years or more. The United States is the new kid on the block. It is only 200 years old, and it has been in Asia just over 100 years. Hence, the relations of Japan and China with the United States are not heavily burdened with history. The United States is also a unique great power, probably the most benevolent great power seen in the history of man. Apart from its colonisation of the Philippines and Cuba, it has had in general no expansionist designs. Indeed, the Asia-Pacific region will be far worse off if the United States leaves than if it stays.

In addition to this benevolence, the United States provides an open Western form of communication, which is more effective than the polite Asian methods, where you never really say what you think.

The Seattle APEC leaders meeting demonstrated the American genius for informality.

PARADOX 5

The fifth paradox is that if we agree that it is in the best interest of China and Japan (and indeed of all East Asian countries) to see the United States retain its presence in the region, then the best way of doing so is for East Asian countries to draw closer to each other.

We saw the value of East Asian cooperation in the early 1990s. Initially the United States was sceptical of APEC (a multilateral arrangement). However, after Malaysia proposed the EAEC, the interest in APEC increased because it was seen as a counter to the EAEC. Similarly, it was good that there was a historic meeting in Kuala Lumpur in December 1997 between ASEAN, China, Japan and Korea. Eventually, if all goes well, the combined GNP of East Asia will become larger than that of North America and Europe combined. East Asian closeness will strengthen the hands of those who argue that the United States should remain engaged and not withdraw from East Asia. This will help to contain isolationism or unilateral tendencies in the United States. The United States is a unique great power as it has the most divided decision-making mechanism at the highest levels. East Asia can stimulate continued US engagement not by drifting apart but by drifting together.

PARADOX 6

The sixth paradox is that while this divided decision-making process of the United States is a source of anxiety or aggravation to many Asian countries, it actually benefits Asia as much as it does the United States. One example of aggravation: China. Despite the US adherence to a one-China policy, Congress passed the Taiwan Relations Act, which contradicts the one-China policy. However, despite their aggravations, East Asian countries should welcome the check and balance of the US system because the net result—usually—is a benevolent US policy.

The main reason why Americans operate with a light touch overseas is that the administration does not have all the power in its hands. Just imagine how the United States would behave if President Clinton had as much power as Stalin. Therefore, Asians should tolerate the annual debate on MFN renewal, on human rights and on trade imbalances because they are part of the noise that goes with the US system. Our challenge is to educate decision makers to restrain themselves in congressional debates.

PARADOX 7

The seventh paradox is that even though it is the United States that is putting up the greatest obstacles to early Chinese membership of the WTO (and this is another controversial statement I am making), it is actually more in the United States' than in China's interest to see a faster Chinese membership in the WTO. The emergence of China as a major economy cannot be stopped. It will become larger and larger. The sooner it plays by international rules, the better it will be for the United States and the international community. Of course, if the United States wants to educate China on how to be a good citizen and play by WTO rules, then it should set an example by re-examining the WTO's inconsistent legislations, such as the Helms Burton Act, the D'Amato Act and so on. Hence, if the United States really studied what was in its long-term interests, it should be doing the exact opposite of what it is doing with China and the WTO and push for early rather than late entry of China into the WTO.

In conclusion, let me hope that I have not confused you about the geopolitical picture of this region with my seven paradoxes. However, as someone who has a ringside seat in the arena of the greatest and the most rapid change in the history of man, I feel that it is my duty to alert you to these surprising developments. My final parting paradox is this: please do not be surprised if you are surprised by developments in our region.

SOUTHEAST ASIA

THE ASEAN "MAGIC"

GAIKO FORUM, APRIL 1996.

The Association of Southeast Asian Nations (ASEAN) is one of the most underrated organisations of contemporary times. When World War II ended and the Southeast Asian states gained independence, most regional experts were pessimistic about the region's future. They warned that Southeast Asia was the "Balkans" of Asia, with greater diversity of race, religion, language, culture, history and geography than even the Balkans of Europe. In the 1960s and 1970s, it would have been foolish to predict that this troubled region would produce the most successful form of regional cooperation outside the European Union. It would have been acknowledged as a miracle if this were to happen. The remarkable thing is that this miracle has occurred and few have noticed it. This essay was published in the journal of the Ministry of Foreign Affairs of Japan.

When a brief history of the 20th century is written, a few towering figures will be mentioned: Stalin and Hitler, Roosevelt and Churchill, Mao Zedong and Deng Xiaoping. Some organisations that may be named are the UN and GATT, EU and NATO, IMF and APEC. Most historians will forget to mention ASEAN. Pity! For, in a quiet way, ASEAN may have done more by improving the lives of the 500 million people of Southeast Asia and, building on this success, reaching out and touching the lives of billions more who live in Asia.

This is an extravagant claim. It will be difficult to prove. And it goes against the grain of Japanese perceptions of ASEAN.

Some years ago, a Japanese professor gave a lecture on ASEAN to a Japanese audience. He likened ASEAN's importance to Japan to that of a salad: a good component of a healthy diet but not essential or vital for Japan's survival. In this salad, he said that Indonesia was like lettuce, the main item in the salad; Brunei like caviar, small but extremely valuable; the Philippines like a red and ripe tomato; Malaysia like avocado; Singapore like red chilli; and Thailand like white asparagus because it gave off "the aroma of culture" (*bunka no kaori o suru*).

This comparison of ASEAN with a salad was an apt analogy to capture its relative importance to Japan in the early years of ASEAN. It was a valid statement to make, especially during the Cold War, when the key dynamics of international relations were influenced by the two superpowers and the other major powers. But as we are now experiencing a major (and so far confusing) transformation of international relations, Japan may find it in its interest to begin to see ASEAN in a new light. A brief three-phase history of ASEAN may explain why.

PHASE 1: THE COLD WAR
ASEAN emerged as a child of the Cold War. It was founded in 1967 in Bangkok, with the ostensible aim of accelerating "the economic growth, social progress and cultural development in the region". But the real

force that brought the ASEAN countries together was a common fear that the five founding members (Indonesia, Malaysia, the Philippines, Singapore and Thailand) had of the communist threat to them. Each had to cope with domestic communist insurgencies, which were then supported, directly or indirectly, by the then two major communist powers, the Soviet Union and the PRC. All ASEAN leaders realised that if they did not work together to foster rapid social and economic development, they could lose the battle to the communists. The wars raging in the neighbouring Indochinese countries provided a daily reminder of the fate that ASEAN countries could encounter if they faltered.

The founders of ASEAN were also aware that the two previous experiments in regional cooperation in Southeast Asia had failed. The Association of Southeast Asia (ASA) was established in 1961 but ran into difficulties soon after its formation, and Maphilindo, composed of Malaysia, the Philippines and Indonesia, was formed in 1963 but aborted even before it got off the ground. This was fortunate for it meant that ASEAN members began the ASEAN experiment with low expectations and therefore proceeded cautiously. No bold experiments were attempted in the early years. Instead, very quietly and without much fanfare, the ASEAN countries planted the seeds for future success by developing habits of cooperation.

It was in these early years that the crucial ASEAN concept of consensus was born. All members realised that ASEAN could not succeed if any of its members tried to dominate the proceedings. Each would have to be sensitive to the interests of others.

Fortunately for all ASEAN members, the largest member of ASEAN, Indonesia (which alone had a population larger than that of the other four founding members), had an indigenous political culture that encouraged consensus. Two Indonesian words, *musyawarah* and *mufakat*, describe the culture. It is hard to translate these words clearly into another language. In essence they suggest that all decisions should be made after careful discussion, after the views of all, big and small, are considered—and that these decisions should reflect the consensus of all.

Indonesia set the tone. It listened patiently to the views of all, refraining from imposing its will despite being the largest member. It genuinely tried to secure consensus. And this notion of consensus became synonymous with ASEAN. No other organisation, not NATO, nor EU, nor the UN nor the Non-Aligned Movement (NAM), has been as faithful to the notion of consensus as ASEAN has been. And this in turn has generated mutual trust and comfort among the members in ASEAN as an organisation.

PHASE 2: THE FALL OF INDOCHINA

The fall of Phnom Penh and Saigon to the communist forces came as a rude shock to the noncommunist members of ASEAN. They were faced with the cold stark reality that a new and more dangerous challenge faced them. It did not help that the new Vietnamese government in Hanoi declared in 1975 that the ASEAN countries had not achieved "genuine independence". This sentiment was echoed by Laos at the 5th Conference of the NAM Heads of State or Government in 1976.

The ASEAN countries reacted swiftly. They stepped up the level of ASEAN cooperation by convening the first ever Summit Meeting of ASEAN Leaders in Bali in 1976 under the chairmanship of President Suharto. Both symbolically and substantively, this was an appropriate move, for it was President Suharto's strong personal commitment to ASEAN that ensured that the Indonesian concept of consensus was practised in ASEAN. The landmark Bali ASEAN Treaty of Amity and Cooperation (which in 1996 still remains valid as the key regional agreement to foster peace and stability) was signed in Bali in 1976.

The shock of 1975 was further aggravated by the Vietnamese invasion of Cambodia in December 1978. This brought Vietnamese tanks right up to the border of an ASEAN member, Thailand. ASEAN was thus forced to make a crucial political decision: to bend and accommodate the new power in Indochina or to take a position of principle and stand up and oppose this occupation of Cambodia by a foreign force. Both impulses were present in ASEAN. History could have gone either way. But the ASEAN countries made the courageous decision to stand on principle on this issue.

This was probably the landmark decision in the history of ASEAN. When the ASEAN countries set about reversing the occupation of Cambodia, the conventional wisdom in most sophisticated political circles was that ASEAN was engaged in a futile exercise. The ASEAN states were acutely aware that the odds were against them, but they persevered. Perseverance in common adversity is an important bonding experience, as soldiers who have fought together in the trenches know so well. Both in the United Nations and in the NAM, the ASEAN states had to learn to cooperate closely to persuade the international community of the rightness of their cause.

History will record that it was these years of extremely close cooperation on the Cambodian issue from 1979 to 1991 (when the Paris Peace Accords on Cambodia were finally signed) that created real bonds of friendship and trust among the ASEAN countries. This in turn fostered a sense of community among the ASEAN member states (which had since grown to six with the admission of Brunei in 1984).

Cooperation among diverse nation-states is never easy. As British Prime Minister Harold Macmillan astutely observed, alliances are held together by fear, not love. The European Union was brought together by the then common fear of the Soviet Union and also the common fear of a return to the two disastrous World Wars that burnt Europe so badly in the first half of the 20th century. ASEAN too was brought together initially by common fears. But, as in Europe, constant cooperation breeds habits of cooperation—and it is these ingrained habits of cooperation that will successfully carry ASEAN through its third and possibly most successful era of cooperation: the post-Cold War era.

PHASE 3: THE POST-COLD WAR ERA

It is not a mere coincidence that the most ambitious effort of ASEAN cooperation was launched at the end of the Cold War—to be precise, exactly three years after the end of the Cold War. This was the landmark decision to launch the ASEAN Free Trade Area at the Fourth ASEAN Summit in Singapore in January 1992.

This was not the first time that the notion of an ASEAN Free Trade Area was suggested. Many such suggestions had been made in earlier years. But they came to nought for a simple reason: there was an insufficiently developed sense of community among the ASEAN states.

The experiences of the EU, NAFTA and CER (between Australia and New Zealand) have demonstrated that free-trade areas can only be successfully established among countries that have already developed a great deal of trust and confidence in each other, and that already have a sense of a common destiny. The countries must first feel that they are rowing the same boat, before they can begin rowing together in the same direction. And, as a corollary, if countries do not feel that they are in the same boat, all regional cooperation will be futile.

Only this vital point can explain why the Balkans of Asia— Southeast Asian countries are often referred to as the "Balkans of Asia" because ethnically, religiously, culturally and historically they are as diverse as, if not more diverse than, the Balkan states of Europe— came together at the precise moment when the Balkans of Europe fell apart in a violent fashion. For a Japanese person to truly understand how far Southeast Asia and ASEAN have come, try to imagine how long it would take to foster the same sense of community and how long it would take to launch a free-trade area in the other half of East Asia, among, say, the neighbouring countries of China, Mongolia, North Korea, South Korea, Russia and Japan. When will there be an ANEAN (Association of North East Asian Nations) to complement ASEAN?

THE ASEAN REGIONAL FORUM (ARF)

ASEAN is acutely aware that it is the only truly successful regional organisation in Asia. Hence, it realises that it has to take the lead in developing a new regional structure to cope with the extremely fluid geopolitical environment that surfaced in East Asia at the end of the Cold War.

Despite its heavy involvement in the Cambodian issue, ASEAN had fought shy of being seen as a political-security organisation. The idea of ASEAN-wide defence cooperation is still taboo (although now at the regular annual "Special" Senior Officials Meeting [SOM], ASEAN defence ministry officials join their foreign ministry colleagues to discuss regional security issues). ASEAN does not want to be perceived as a reincarnation of the Southeast Asia Treaty Organisation (SEATO) or an Asian equivalent of NATO. It has not been, is not, and possibly never will be, a military alliance. (In any case, the general track record of military alliances or military blocs, with the possible exception of NATO, has not been outstanding.)

However, when the ASEAN leaders met at the Singapore Summit in January 1992, they realised that there was no choice. Japan had tried, at the July 1991 ASEAN-PMC, to launch an initiative for region-wide security discussions, but the effort did not take off. Similarly, in 1990 Australian foreign minister Gareth Evans had also proposed the creation of an Asian version of the Conference of Security and Cooperation to address regional security problems.

ASEAN realised that it was only an ASEAN invitation that could draw all the major powers to sit together to discuss security matters in the Asia-Pacific because only ASEAN enjoyed the confidence of all the major powers as an impartial organisation. This is why the Singapore Summit Declaration of 1992 stated that ASEAN would intensify its dialogues on "political and security matters".

This decision was finally translated into reality when ASEAN organised a dinner during the 1993 ASEAN Ministerial Meeting in Singapore to plant the idea of a regional forum to discuss security issues. The dinner was attended by all the prospective members of the ASEAN Regional Forum (ARF). The ARF was formally created a year later in Bangkok. The ARF is a unique forum that brings ASEAN and its observers, dialogue partners and consultative partners together. When the ARF meets, all the major powers of the world (the United States, Russia, China, Europe, Japan and, soon, India) gather in one room to address regional security issues.

The remarkable thing is the high level of comfort in the room, even though many of the participants (including the major powers) have many outstanding bilateral problems. The reason is simple: ASEAN has invented a particular kind of "magic" to keep regional cooperation going in a region that is so easily Balkanised. But after having developed this magic over the course of 28 years, ASEAN is now in a position to share it with the larger Asia-Pacific region.

The best example of ASEAN's magic is its ability to absorb Vietnam as a member in 1995, barely four years after ending a decade-long tussle with the latter over Cambodia. Neither the ASEAN states nor Vietnam changed their domestic political systems. But Vietnam's decision to join the free market system and to support ASEAN's vision of a peaceful, stable and prosperous Southeast Asia qualifies it for membership. ASEAN continues to progress smoothly after the inclusion of Vietnam. The Fifth ASEAN Summit in Bangkok in December 1995 (with Vietnam present) has proven to be the most successful ASEAN summit so far, with bold proposals emerging to push Southeast Asian and East Asian cooperation even further. And Vietnam boldly announced that it would host the Sixth Formal ASEAN Summit in 1998. Contrast this ASEAN record with the problems that both EU and NATO faced in absorbing the members of the former Soviet bloc in Europe. This gives a good indication of the magic that ASEAN has created to generate faster regional cooperation.

Japan should welcome this. It now has friendly relations with all its neighbours—Russia, South Korea and China. But Japan also has difficulties and outstanding problems with them that prevent the development of an Association of Northeast Asian Nations (ANEAN). If the ASEAN magic of peace, stability and prosperity spreads throughout the Asia-Pacific region, all the countries, including Japan, will benefit from it.

In short, ASEAN's success and durability should, therefore, be seen as a vital, not peripheral, national interest of Japan. Japanese professors should stop viewing ASEAN as a mere salad. They should now compare it to gourmet cuisine like *kaiseki ryori*, or other delectable dishes like *sashimi* and *sushi*, which the Japanese could not imagine living without.

POL POT: THE PARADOX OF MORAL CORRECTNESS

TERRORISM, VOLUME 16, 1993.

It is a historical curiosity that Cambodia, a country of 7 million people, could produce one of the evil giants of the 20th century, almost on a par with Hitler and Stalin. When the Vietnamese army removed Pol Pot from power in December 1978, the world applauded. But when it decided to remain in Cambodia as an army of invasion and occupation, an acute moral dilemma was created: to work with Pol Pot to remove the Vietnamese occupation or not. Most Cambodians and Southeast Asians chose to work with Pol Pot, on the same grounds that Churchill had chosen to work with Stalin against Hitler, but every major Western newspaper and journal condemned the partnership. This essay tries to spell out the paradoxically harmful consequences of such morally correct postures that were the fashion among Western intellectuals in the 1980s. Significantly, such moral correctness dissipated when Western intellectuals had to cope directly with morally complex situations in places such as Bosnia and Chechnya. Still, I was surprised no Western Op-Ed guru dared to articulate the views suggested in this essay.

It was August 1942, a dark moment in World War II. Churchill had flown secretly to Moscow to bring some bad news personally to Stalin: the Allies were not ready for a second front in Europe. Stalin reacted angrily. Nancy Caldwell Sorel, who describes that meeting, writes:

> Discord continued, but on the last evening, when Churchill went to say goodbye, Stalin softened … the hour that Churchill had planned for extended to seven. Talk and wine flowed freely, and in a moment of rare intimacy, Stalin admitted that even the stresses of war did not compare to the terrible struggle to force the collective farm policy on the peasantry. Millions of Kulaks had been, well, eliminated. The historian Churchill thought of Burke's dictum "If I cannot have reform without justice, I will not have reform," but the politician Churchill concluded that with the war requiring unity, it was best not to moralize aloud.[1]

The story elicits a chuckle. What a shrewd old devil Churchill was. How cunning of him not to displease Stalin with mere moralising. Neither then nor now has Churchill's reputation been sullied by his association with a genocidal ruler. Now change the cast of characters to an identical set: Margaret Thatcher and Pol Pot. Historically they could have met, but of course they never did. Now try to describe a possible meeting and try to get a chuckle out of it. Impossible? Why?

Think about it. Think hard, for in doing so you will discover to your surprise that it is possible for thoughtful and well-informed people to have double standards. If the rule that prevents any possible meeting between Thatcher and Pol Pot is that "thou shalt not have any discourse with a genocidal ruler," then the same rule also forbids any meeting between Stalin and Churchill. Moral rules, as the English philosopher R. M. Hare has stressed, are inherently universalisable. If we do want to allow a meeting between Churchill and Stalin (since historians do not condemn Churchill, that must be the prevailing sentiment), then the rule has to be modified to "thou shalt not have any discourse with a genocidal ruler, unless there are mitigating circumstances."

This is not a mere change of nuance. We have made a fundamental leap. In Churchill's case, as England's survival was at stake, all was excused. In Pol Pot's case, as no conceivable vital Western interest could be served in any meeting with him, no mitigating excuse could possibly exist for an equally flexible Western relationship with Pol Pot as with Stalin. Hence the total Western condemnation of any direct contact with Pol Pot or his minions in the Khmer Rouge. The tragedy for the Cambodian people is that the West, in applying this strict rule because its *own* vital interests were not involved, did not stop to ask whether the sufferings of the *Cambodians* could have been mitigated if the West had been as flexible in their dealings with the Khmer Rouge as Churchill had been with Stalin.

These attitudes have caused considerable difficulties for the Western policymakers (in both Western Europe and North America) on Cambodia. Their attempts to fashion pragmatic solutions for the Cambodian problem (pragmatic solutions that necessarily have to *include* the Khmer Rouge) have been excoriated by their press and parliamentarians in favour of morally pure policies *excluding* the Khmer Rouge. Curiously, these moral pursuits would also have opposed any Western military involvement against the Khmer Rouge, especially any new American military intervention in Indochina, leaving one to ask: if you cannot eliminate them and you do not include them, how would it be possible to have a peace agreement? Without a peace agreement, how can you end Cambodia's agony and ensure its future as an independent state?

NGUYEN CO THACH

Someday, historians enjoying the same access to Vietnamese archives as we do now to Soviet archives might be able to document that the Vietnamese leaders, especially Nguyen Co Thach, a brilliant tactician, were able to exploit these Western attitudes to the hilt. He certainly did so at the Paris Peace Conference in August 1989. It is questionable whether that conference could have ever succeeded, given the hardline leaders still in power in Hanoi then. Nevertheless, Nguyen Co Thach chose a brilliant tactic to scuttle the conference, a tactic which the West found hard to challenge.

Towards the end of the conference, he insisted that the conference declaration should explicitly call for the non-return of the genocidal policies and practices of the Khmer Rouge. All present knew that in reality Nguyen Co Thach was not that concerned about Pol Pot's record. (Indeed, Thach once made the mistake of privately confessing to congressman Stephen Solarz that Vietnam did *not* invade Cambodia to save the Cambodian people from Pol Pot, even though this was the official Vietnamese propaganda line.) However, Thach knew that the Khmer Rouge, a party to the Paris conference, would not accept such a reference. Hence, the conference would fail, a failure that the Vietnamese wanted because they were not ready then to relinquish control of Cambodia. Western officials did not dare to challenge him for fear of being branded defenders of Pol Pot by Nguyen Co Thach. In practical terms, from the viewpoint of the ordinary Cambodian, the strong Western consensus against the Khmer Rouge had backfired and ruined any chance of agreement because it prevented Western delegations from exposing Nguyen Co Thach's scuttling of the peace conference. Out of good (the Western condemnation of Pol Pot) came evil (the destruction of a peace conference). This was not the first time it had happened in history. As Max Weber said in his famous essay, "it is *not* true that good can only follow from good and evil only from evil, but that often the opposite is true. Anyone who says this is, indeed, a political infant."[2]

The morally courageous thing for a Western delegate to have done at that Paris conference would have been to stand up at a press conference and explain why the inclusion of the Khmer Rouge was necessary *if one wanted a peace agreement to end the Cambodians' sufferings*. No Western leader even dreamt of doing so, so strong was the sentiment against the Khmer Rouge. This produced a curious contradiction for moral philosophers: the ostensibly morally correct position (that of excluding the Khmer Rouge) produced immoral consequences—prolonging Cambodia's agony.

This was not by any means the first of such moral dilemmas confronted by Western officials. Weber's essay, mentioned above, notes that all politicians, statesmen and officials will experience a tension between what he calls "an ethic of ultimate ends" and "an ethic of responsibility". Even more boldly, Weber asserts, "No ethics in the world can dodge the fact that in numerous instances the attainment of 'good' ends is bound to the fact that one must be willing to pay the price of using morally dubious means or at least dangerous ones."[3] In the search for the "good" of peace for the Cambodian people, Weber would have certainly understood why in practical terms Western officials had to deal with the Khmer Rouge.

ROLE OF WESTERN PUBLIC OPINION

This could well be a fascinating issue for future historians to study: why did Western pubic opinion not realise that its moral campaign against the Khmer Rouge was being used to immoral ends by others? It is equally surprising that many in the West were prepared to accept the Vietnamese claim that they provided the bulwark against the return of the Khmer Rouge when it was the Vietnamese military intervention in Cambodia in the early 1970s that paved the way for Pol Pot to gain power in Phnom Penh. This can be documented. It was the North Vietnamese army that decimated Lon Nol's army and paved the way for the youthful and relatively inexperienced Khmer Rouge forces to take over Cambodia. The Vietnamese praised Pol Pot's rule right up until the moment that they invaded. When they removed Pol Pot from power, they installed former Khmer Rouge cadres in his place.

There is absolutely no doubt that both Pol Pot and the Khmer Rouge deserve all the ignominy heaped upon them. Someday they should be brought to justice. The Vietnamese did the Cambodian people a great favour by removing Pol Pot. All this is true. It is equally true that the sole Vietnamese motive in invading Cambodia was to fulfil a long-standing historical ambition to establish hegemony over Indochina. Through the 1980s many Cambodians agreed that Cambodia faced the threat of extinction as an independent nation. Hence, they reluctantly accepted Pol Pot's argument that without the Khmer Rouge the Cambodian nation that had once almost disappeared in the face of Vietnamese expansionism in the 19th century might not survive in the 20th century. Pol Pot may have been adept at exploiting a deep-seated Cambodian fear for his own political purposes, but one reason he could do so is that many in the West, insensitive to Cambodian history, insisted that the West should merely recognise the Vietnamese-installed regime of Hun Sen. In the eyes of many Cambodians, acceptance of Vietnamese occupation could have meant the extinction of the Cambodian nation. That was the fundamental reason why many worked with Pol Pot, directly or indirectly.

In short, what these Cambodians did in working with Pol Pot was what Churchill did in working with Stalin—work with a genocidal ruler for national survival. Yet all Cambodians who once worked with Pol Pot were vilified, including Prince Sihanouk (but not Hun Sen). Few stepped back to consider for a minute whether these Cambodians had a legitimate fear that unless they worked with Pol Pot to end the Vietnamese occupation, Cambodia would disappear as a nation and the Cambodian people end up like the Kurds. Many Cambodians understood this possibility well. This is what happened to a minority group in Cambodia, the Chams, who had been driven into Cambodia and out of their homeland by Vietnamese expansionism in previous centuries. The Cambodians did not want to suffer the same fate.

From the viewpoint of the Cambodians, the ferocious Western crusade against Pol Pot and his Khmer Rouge had many paradoxical aspects. On the one hand it demonstrated the enormous Western concern over the fate of the Cambodians. Many of those who took part in these campaigns were well intentioned. However, in the great Western concern that the Khmer Rouge should be eliminated at all costs (but *without* any overt Western military involvement), they failed to see that this campaign was being exploited by those whom the Cambodians considered equally or more dangerous in the long run: the Vietnamese. The underlying attitude towards the Cambodians in many newspaper editorials was "we know that Hun Sen is imperfect but as he is the best available, take him." It would have been fair for a Cambodian to respond: would any Western society accept such potentially lethal colonisation for themselves?

Unfortunately for the Cambodians, their own problems with the Vietnamese may have been unwittingly caught up in a peculiar problem in the American psyche, the hangover from the Vietnam War. Their age-old problem with Vietnamese expansionism in Indochina (an expansionism as natural as the United States' expansionism into Mexican territory) somehow became entangled with the efforts of many Americans to come to terms with their own involvement in Indochina, especially with their assessments of Vietnam.

This meant that the questions that the Cambodians posed were not posed in the West. For example, it would be reasonable for the Cambodians to ask: would Cambodia have been better off if the antiwar movement had not succeeded? Would there have been no Pol Pot then? The record of those who remained silent in the Nazi holocaust has been well studied. But the record of those who encouraged the forces that led to Pol Pot's takeover in 1975 has not even been touched. It is still too sensitive.

Would it be fair for the Cambodians to pose this question: if there had been no hangover from the Vietnam War and if some in the West were not looking for ways to justify to themselves their support for North Vietnam during the Vietnam War, would as many in the West have latched on so quickly to the Vietnamese argument that they had gone into Cambodia to save the Cambodian people from the Khmer Rouge? Looking dispassionately at the events in 1978–79 leading up to the Vietnamese invasion, it was clear that Cambodia had once again become a pawn in a complex power struggle involving the Soviet Union, China and Vietnam. However, instead of focusing on the victim's plight in being caught once again in a power struggle of giants, much of the Western media focused on the Khmer Rouge issue, thereby tacitly condoning the Vietnamese invasion of Cambodia. The Cambodians found themselves in a bizarre situation where many in the West were trying to rescue them from yesterday's plight while the then ongoing power game involving Cambodia as a pawn continued unabated and under-reported.

THE UN PEACE AGREEMENT

It is something of a miracle that despite the public distortion of some of the key issues involved, a comprehensive peace agreement was reached on Cambodia in October 1991. In one of the greatest historical ironies of the 20th century, all those who tried to use Cambodia as a pawn came to grief: the Soviet Union, China and Vietnam. By late 1991, all wanted to release Cambodia from their grip. The agreement was both brilliant and simple. To "save face" (an Asian requirement) of each of the key protagonists, no one was perceived to be the victor. In place of the then two claimants of Cambodian sovereignty, a nominal Supreme National Council was created to serve as the legal repository of Cambodian sovereignty; but effective power would be handed over to a UN administration that would run the country and enable it to reach a certain degree of normalcy until UN-supervised elections could be held. A ceasefire took effect as soon as the agreement was signed. All the military forces in Cambodia would be regrouped and cantoned and 70 percent of them eventually would be disarmed. External military supplies would cease. Most importantly, as the Cambodians would not vote for the Khmer Rouge (present or former cadres) in free and impartial elections, this would effectively prevent the return to power of the Khmer Rouge and consign them to the same fate as all the other communist parties of the noncommunist states in Southeast Asia as spent forces left to languish in the jungles.

The peace agreement was a wonderful development. Almost immediately after its signing it opened a new chapter in Southeast

Asian history, beginning a process of reconciliation among the long-divided ASEAN and Indochinese states. Every state in the region supported it. Yet after its signing, the Cambodian people found themselves again a victim of Western contradictions.

Under the provisions of the agreement, two Khmer Rouge delegates returned to Phnom Penh in December 1991. Some demonstrations were organised against their return to Phnom Penh. Violence flared out of control. One of the Khmer Rouge delegates, Khieu Samphan, was almost hanged. In their reporting and analysis of this event, almost all the Western media claimed that these were *spontaneous* demonstrations against the Khmer Rouge, failing to ask the obvious question—how could spontaneous demonstrations suddenly surface? The editorials focused on how terrible it was that the Khmer Rouge were again being foisted on the Cambodian people. A *Washington Post* editorial (Sunday, 1 December 1991) said, for example, "Forgetting the past means forgetting the people who were murdered. That is precisely what the Cambodian people are unable and, to their credit, unwilling to do." These papers could not and did not report the real truth: forces in the Hun Sen regime were trying to scuttle an agreement that would eventually kill not just the Khmer Rouge (who would have great difficulty winning UN-supervised elections) but also the Hun Sen regime, who feared the ballot box almost as much.

Fortunately, in this particular incident, the truth was to surface a few months later. The *New Yorker* carried an extensive description that revealed how the whole incident was stage-managed by the Hun Sen regime. The article said, "While Cambodians had every justification for rising up in anger and attacking the Khmer Rouge compound, the fact is that nothing in Cambodia happens spontaneously."[4] The day before Khieu Samphan's return students at the Phnom Penh University were given placards written by Hun Sen's Ministry of Interior and told to go and demonstrate against the return of the Khmer Rouge. When the actual attacks on Khieu Samphan occurred, only 20 or 30 young men, speaking Cambodian with Vietnamese accents, were involved.

They were far outnumbered by the policemen and soldiers present. Instead of restraining the attackers, the policemen helped them along. How could the dozens of Western reporters who were present in Phnom Penh then get their story so wrong? Were they afraid that in reporting the truth they would do the Khmer Rouge a favour? How could they have failed to notice that the demonstrations would help those trying to scuttle the peace process, a point, as the *New Yorker* article points out, that was obvious to the Cambodian students? Only the *Economist* (7 December 1991, p. 14) was brave enough to say that those who supported the peace agreement should defend the continued presence of the Khmer Rouge delegates in Phnom Penh, until elections were held.

That dangerous moment passed. The Khmer Rouge delegates returned to Phnom Penh. The correlation of external forces that wanted peace in Cambodia prevailed on the Hun Sen regime to cease its mischief. The UN peace agreement is back on track. Yet it is more than likely that other such dangerous moments will arise until peace is finally restored to Cambodia.

Some American congressmen have threatened to withhold funding for the UN peace plan on the grounds that it confers "political and moral legitimacy upon the Khmer Rouge" and that it "relies too heavily upon Khmer Rouge cooperation for its success."[5] Their intention is to rescue the Cambodians from the Khmer Rouge. But if they succeed in cutting off the funding, the peace plan would disappear, war would resume, and the Khmer Rouge would be back in their element. Once again, if these congressmen succeed, the morally correct position would lead to disaster for the Cambodians. Elizabeth Becker has wisely reminded them that in 1975 it was the congressional decision to "cut back American aid to the Phnom Penh regime," on the grounds that it "would bring peace more swiftly to Cambodia," that led to the Khmer Rouge victory.[6] The Cambodians earnestly hope that Congress will not repeat the mistake it made in 1975.

MORAL OUTRAGE VERSUS CLINICAL TREATMENT

When a new disease or plague emerges, even out of human neglect or wilfulness, any moral outrage against its emergence would be accompanied by dispassionate and clinical analysis to find both its cause and cure. The Khmer Rouge represent no less than a plague on Cambodian society. The outrage has surfaced. The clinical analysis has not, creating yet another moral paradox. How could all those who were so outraged by the Khmer Rouge not devote equal time to finding effective solutions to stamp out the Khmer Rouge?

The Left, in both its old and new forms, fought the hardest against any dispassionate analysis of the Khmer Rouge, accusing any poor soul who tried to do so of moral insensitivity. There was a reason for this virulent behaviour. The Left has a powerful vested interest in portraying the Khmer Rouge as a unique pathological phenomenon, not linked to any other leftist movements. The truth, however, is that Pol Pot represents not a unique disease but only the most extreme form of a common plague mankind has seen: the plague of communism. The fundamental mistake that Pol Pot and his colleagues made was to interpret Marx and Lenin literally. When these founders of the communist movement called for the extermination of the bourgeoisie, Pol Pot assumed that this meant physical elimination, not just their elimination as a political force. In their early years of power, Pol Pot and his colleagues took great pride that the purest form of communism in the world was to be found in Cambodia. Further dispassionate analysis of the origins of Pol Pot will also show that he could never have come to power on his own. He was propelled into Phnom Penh on the back of the Vietnamese revolution, which in turn received massive support from both the Soviet Union and China.

Such dispassionate analysis actually produces hope for the Cambodian people on at least four counts. First, if Pol Pot was swept into power in Phnom Penh with the high tide of communism, his chances of getting back into power are slim because this high tide has receded. Pol Pot and his movement survive like a few marine species stranded in a small pool left behind on the beach, far from the receded shoreline. If the tide does not come back to claim them, they are doomed in a hostile environment. Southeast Asia represents such a hostile environment. It experienced many huge waves of communist expansionism, with communist parties running riot in virtually all Southeast Asian societies. Today the pathetic relics that remain in Thailand, Malaysia or Indonesia survive only as spent forces. Eventually, the Khmer Rouge will share the same fate. The tide of history is against them.

Second, the correlation of forces, to use a favourite Marxist expression, that propelled Pol Pot into Phnom Penh cannot be re-created. Instead, the new correlation of forces favours their eventual extinction if only because all of their supporters in the 1970s, the Soviet Union, China and Vietnam, each for their own reasons, want to see the effective implementation of the UN Cambodian peace agreement. This correlation of forces should be exploited by those implementing the UN peace agreement. If either the Khmer Rouge or the Hun Sen regime violate the peace agreement, their respective patrons should be held accountable for their behaviour.

Third, if both Pol Pot and his offshoot, the Hun Sen regime, represent nothing more than versions of communist rule, their behaviour can be *predicted*. Communism is not a new phenomenon. There is enough evidence available on the methods that communists use to gain power. Under Leninist rules, all is justified in the fight for power. Lying and cheating are routine. Both the Khmer Rouge and the Hun Sen regime have already demonstrated this in the early days of the UN plan. The Khmer Rouge are violating the peace accords by denying the UN access to territories under their control. The Hun Sen regime (although it is divided) is violating the accords by unleashing its thugs to wipe out or intimidate Cambodians trying to form new political parties. The media reports have expressed surprise that this should have happened. A basic book on communist tactics should have told them what was going to happen. The UN should employ a few experienced anti-communist tacticians to help it anticipate the political behaviour of the Cambodian communists. Their mindset is known; therefore, the behaviour can be predicted.

Fourth, and finally, intelligent tactics should be used against the Khmer Rouge. If the Khmer Rouge believe that the UN plan will be rigged against them in the implementation process, they will only fight like cornered rats, giving no quarter, spilling even more blood. However, if they are convinced that the UN plan will be implemented fairly and impartially, they may give it a try. The Khmer Rouge leaders believe, contrary to Western perceptions, that they still enjoy political support for at least two reasons. First, they represent the least corrupted force in Cambodia. Second, with their impressive anti-Vietnamese credentials, they can portray themselves as true nationalists, as they are trying to do.

Extending the analogy of the beached marine species, there is nothing that would kill these species more than exposure to the open sun. Hence, they will make every effort to look for rocks under which to hide. In the case of the Khmer Rouge, the best tactic would be to lure them out from under the rocks and into the open political environment, where they and their supporters will face both the Cambodian population and the international community. They must be made to feel safe to emerge. The subdued response of the international community to the attempted lynching of Khieu Samphan sent the wrong message to the Khmer Rouge, that the international community would not protest strongly if other Cambodian parties violated the agreement. This will drive them farther away from the sunlight.

It will be emotionally difficult for some of the Western officials involved in the UN operations to be strictly impartial in dealing with the Khmer Rouge. The temptation to work against them, or to remain silent when the Phnom Penh regime attacks the Khmer Rouge, will be strong. But nothing could imperil the peace agreement more than the perception that it was not being fairly implemented. One should always bear in mind that the best poison pill that could be administered to the Khmer Rouge and guarantee their eventual disappearance from the Cambodian scene is the open, impartial and effective implementation of the UN peace agreement. When all the Cambodian armed forces are disarmed and cantoned, and when the citizens of Phnom Penh feel that they can speak freely and not fear assassination attempts, as they do now, from some thugs sent out by the Phnom Penh regime, then a new political chemistry will emerge on the Cambodian scene. In this new political chemistry, Cambodian society will go along with the global trend and reject all forms of communism, whether it be the Pol Pot or Hun Sen variety. The anomalous situation today, where the strongest and best-financed Cambodian forces are the communist groups, will then end.

CONCLUSION

Through 1992 and 1993 the Cambodians will earnestly hope and pray that the imperilled UN peace plan will be successfully implemented and deliver them from two decades of agony. Their fate hangs on its successful implementation. If it fails, it will rob the Cambodians of effectively their last chance of deliverance from decades of suffering. Under these circumstances, the Cambodians could well pose these questions: Why did the ferocious Western campaign against the Khmer Rouge, which elevated Pol Pot to the great historical ranks of Hitler and Stalin while he (Pol Pot) was still alive, have so little *practical* effect on the Cambodian people? Why did the Cambodian problem take so long to be solved even though it became one of the most powerful symbols of 20th century tragedy in the Western mind at a time when the West was globally dominant? Why did Western governments find it so difficult to pay for the UN peace operations when both their citizens and media were so exercised by the Cambodian tragedy? Even more curiously, at the precise historical moment when capitalism declared its victory over communism, the two best-financed Cambodian political forces remained the communist forces: the Khmer Rouge through their access to the Pailin diamond mines, and the Hun Sen regime through their ability to raise money in a corrupt fashion in Phnom Penh. Why did the two noncommunist forces find so much difficulty in raising matching funds in the West? Why did the ferocious Western media campaign against the Khmer Rouge help the Cambodian people so little? What was the moral value of championing moral causes *without* paying much heed to the consequences of these campaigns? This may not have been the first time that it has occurred. To quote Weber one last time, "If, however, one chases after the ultimate good in a war of beliefs, following a pure ethic of absolute ends, then the goals may be damaged and discredited for generations, because responsibility for *consequences* is lacking, and the diabolic forces which enter the play remain unknown to the actor."[7]

Perhaps the best response that the West can give to all these questions is to cease its efforts to find morally pure solutions for the Cambodian people and instead concentrate on ensuring that the UN peace plan is effectively and fully implemented. When that is done Cambodia could well be transformed from a symbol of tragedy to a symbol of hope in the 20th century and the Western conscience would be fully assuaged.

1. Nancy Caldwell Sorel, "First Encounters: Josef Stalin and Winston Churchill", *The Atlantic Monthly*, November 1991, p. 141.
2. Max Weber, *Politics As a Vocation*, Philadelphia, Fortress Press, 1965, p. 49.
3. Ibid., p. 47.
4. Stan Sesser, "Report from Cambodia", *The New Yorker*, 18 May 1992, p. 48.
5. Elizabeth Becker, "Up from Hell", *The New Republic*, 7 February 1992, p. 33.
6. Ibid., p. 36.
7. Weber, op. cit., p. 53.

MISCELLANEOUS

SINGAPORE: RECIPES FOR A CROWDED PLANET

SCHEDULED TO APPEAR IN THE UNDP HUMAN DEVELOPMENT REPORT,

AUTUMN 1998.

When Singapore gained independence in 1965, its leaders cried rather than cheered. The idea that a small island city-state of 2 million people with no hinterland could survive in what was then a difficult and troubled region seemed manifestly absurd. The odds were always against Singapore succeeding. The remarkable thing is not only that it has succeeded against the odds; rather, it is that the country has actually become one of the most successful developing nations in the world. Not all of Singapore's successful development experience is relevant to the rest of the world, but parts of it clearly are. Hence, when the editors of the 1998 annual UNDP Human Development Report asked me to prepare a short note on Singapore's experience, I was happy to do so.

As we approach the end of the 20th century, a growing concern in many minds around the globe is that we live on an overpopulated and ecologically threatened planet. In 100 years, the earth's population has trebled from 1.6 billion in 1900 to a projected 5.25 billion in 2000, creating a global average of 35 persons per square kilometre. Bangladesh, a modern metaphor for overpopulation, has 855 persons per square kilometre. However, the most crowded country in the world is Singapore, with 4,630 persons per square kilometre.

Singapore ought not to have succeeded. The odds were always against it. The 2 million people squeezed on an island of 648 square kilometres (a quarter the size of Luxembourg), with no natural resources, had little going for them. Their success in overcoming the odds and, along the way, finding innovative social and economic solutions may offer some suggestions to those concerned about a crowded planet.

The relative economic success of Singapore is probably well known. Its economy has grown by over 7 percent per annum since independence in 1965, leading to a per capita income of US$31,140 (ranked sixth in the world). Some maintain that Singapore has the most efficient port, airport, airline and civil service in the world. It also has the third largest oil refining capability and one of the largest financial centres. Its total trade is three times the size of its GNP. The policy prescriptions created to achieve this were relatively simple: sustain a free and open economy, avoid any subsidy, welcome foreign investment and aim for budgetary surpluses. The values of hard work and thrift, and the virtues of increasing worker productivity, were always emphasised.

Hidden behind this economic story, however, is another story that is surprisingly little known. Societies should be judged ultimately on their ability to deliver to their citizens most of their human needs: food, shelter, health, education, a clean environment, a sense of community and a sense of purpose in life. It is on these dimensions that Singapore could perhaps provide recipes for a crowded planet.

The socio-economic policies of Singapore are difficult to characterise. They fit neither the capitalist nor the socialist paradigm. Instead, a healthy pragmatic spirit and an openness to innovation and experience characterise the approach of the government. Food is cheap and plentiful because imports are encouraged from all over the world. Singapore produces none at home, but the average worker can buy lunch for two to three US dollars. Shelter is also plentiful. Ninety percent of the population live in high-rise public housing that occupies only one-sixth of the island. The average dwelling space per family is above the global average. Virtually all Singaporeans live in homes they own because of a compulsory savings programme (the Central Provident Fund [CPF]). A worker earning US$1,000 a month (and many do earn this much) would save at least US$400 every month: US$200 from his salary and US$200 from a matching employers' contribution. Their investment in housing has paid off, because the average flat has trebled in value over the past 10 years.

The CPF scheme also enables most Singaporeans to save for medical expenses. The health system has moved away from full government subsidy to increasing co-payment. However, no one who needs medical treatment is denied it, because of three-tier protection: personal savings through Medisave, a government low-cost insurance scheme through Medishield, and government assistance through Medifund. The population has become healthier every year. Infant mortality rates have fallen from 26.3 per 1,000 births in 1965 to 4 per 1,000 today. Life expectancy is rising. Education is neither totally free nor compulsory, but today 90 percent of each cohort will complete at least 10 years of education; 20 percent will complete university; 40 percent will complete polytechnic training; and 30 percent will complete vocational training. Early educational streaming ensures that the different talents are recognised and developed from an early age.

The story on the environment front is also worth studying. Long before the Green movement surfaced, the then prime minister, Lee Kuan Yew, said: "I have always believed that a blighted urban landscape, a concrete jungle, destroys the human spirit. We need the greenery of nature to lift our spirits." With careful land planning, only 49 percent of the island is used for residential, commercial and industrial purposes. Hence, half the island consists of forest reserves, water catchment areas, marshes and other non-built up areas. It is a green island, even though the World Bank classifies the population as "one hundred percent urbanised". Curiously, there is more biodiversity in Singapore than in all of the United States.

From the early days, Singapore recognised the threat posed by cars. Hence, both ownership and usage of cars are severely taxed. To buy a car, one has to first buy a piece of paper—a Certificate of Entitlement (COE). A limited number of COEs are auctioned every month, to control car population growth. Today an average COE costs US$30,000. Including taxes, a Mercedes-Benz now costs over US$150,000. In 1998 an Electronic Road Pricing Scheme (ERPS) was launched to control car usage and manage traffic congestion. This penalisation of car transport is balanced by the provision of efficient subway and bus services, which, surprisingly, are not subsidised. Bus companies make money because the word "subsidy" is virtually taboo in Singapore.

This careful attention to meeting the physical and material needs of the population is matched by equal care and concern for the people's social and spiritual needs. In this, however, Singapore has consciously moved away from the welfare state prescriptions of OECD societies. There are no homeless, destitute or starving people in Singapore. Poverty has been eradicated, not through an entitlements programme (there are virtually none), but through a unique partnership between the government, corporate citizens, self-help groups and voluntary initiatives. The state acts as the catalyst—matching financial support, sponsoring preventive and social care, and ensuring that basic needs are provided for. Remarkably, the poorest 5 percent of households have about the same levels of ownership of homes, television sets, refrigerators, telephones, washing machines and video recorders as the national average. Perhaps this, combined with the tough law and order regime, explains why Singapore has one of the lowest crime rates in the world—167 per 100,000.

Singaporean society emphasises the importance of the family. Government policies are skewed in favour of encouraging extended families to live in the same neighbourhood. These policies also encourage families to care for their own elderly. The traditional Asian emphasis on clan and kinship provides a valuable social glue, even as society modernises and develops.

An equally strong emphasis is placed on multiracial harmony, given the experience with racial riots before independence. The government publishes notices in the four official languages (Mandarin, Malay, Tamil and English). Every Singaporean child has to be bilingual, and there is no ethnic discrimination in school or in the civil service. To avoid the evolution of racial ghettoes in public housing, all estates are required to have a certain percentage of minority population. Citizen and community groups are encouraged to be multiracial. Every constituency is also provided with a community centre, open to all citizens. A dense network of citizen consultative groups enables citizens to participate in managing the affairs of their community.

Singapore is not a perfect society. Nor is it a paradise. Affluence has created bad social habits: excessive consumption and waste generation. According to the UNEP, Singaporeans generated 1.1 kg of domestic waste per person per day, compared to Germany's 0.9 kg. Littering lingers as a bad habit. Singapore is also not spared from the social problems of modern cities—drug abuse, juvenile delinquency, vandalism and teenage crime—even though the deterrents are severe.

The struggle for survival and social improvement will be an eternal one for Singapore. But the few successes that the country has had may carry a message of hope. If the rest of the world could agree to accept the living conditions of Singaporeans, then the 5.25 billion people of our planet may need only an area the size of South Africa to live in. Somehow, this possibility does make the planet appear less crowded.

THE TEN COMMANDMENTS FOR DEVELOPING COUNTRIES IN THE NINETIES

ENVIRONMENT GUARDIAN, 21 SEPTEMBER 1990.

In 1990 I was invited to attend the regular annual UNDP conference in Antalya, Turkey, a truly beautiful corner of the world. I knew little about developmental theory, but I did know that the conventional developmental theory that had been passed on to Third World societies had truly not worked well in developing them. Indeed, the real tragedy of many developing countries was that after the immediate euphoria of independence of colonial rule, they found the business of self-government to be difficult. A few progressed. Many slid backwards. It seemed to me unfair and unjust that Third World minds continued to be dished out conventional wisdom that had not worked in practice. Hence, I decided to offer some unconventional thoughts on development. To my surprise, these thoughts travelled well. They were published in many magazines and also in *Change: Threat or Opportunity for Human Progress*, edited by Uner Kirdar, Vol. II, United Nations, New York, 1992.

1. Thou shalt blame only thyself for thine failures in development. Blaming imperialism, colonialism and neo-imperialism is a convenient excuse to avoid self-examination.

2. Thou shalt acknowledge that corruption is the single most important cause for failures in development. Developed countries are not free from corruption, but with their affluence they can afford to indulge in savings and loan scandals.

3. Thou shalt not subsidise any products. Nor punish the farmer to favour the city dweller. High prices are the only effective signal to increase production. If there are food riots, thou shalt resign from office.

4. Thou shalt abandon state control for free markets. Thou shalt have faith in thine own population. An alive and productive population naturally causes development.

5. Thou shalt borrow no more. Thou shalt get foreign investment that pays for itself. Thou shalt build only the infrastructure that is needed and create no white elephants nor railways that end in deserts. Thou shalt accept no aid that is intended only to subsidise ailing industries in developed countries.

6. Thou shalt not reinvent the wheel. Millions of people have gone through the path of development. Take the well-travelled roads. Be not prisoners of dead ideologies.

7. Thou shalt scrub the ideas of Karl Marx out of thine minds and replace them with the ideas of Adam Smith. The Germans have made their choice. Thou shalt follow suit.

8. Thou shalt be humble when developing and not lecture the developed world on their sins. They listened politely in the 1960s and 1970s. They no longer will in the 1990s.

9. Thou shalt abandon all North-South forums, which only encourage hypocritical speeches and token gestures. Thou shalt remember that the countries that have received the greatest amount of aid per capita have failed most spectacularly in development. Thou shalt throw out all theories of development.

10. Thou shalt not abandon hope. People are the same the world over. What Europe achieved yesterday, the developing world will achieve tomorrow. It can be done.

ABOUT THE AUTHOR

A student of philosophy and history, Kishore Mahbubani has published extensively in leading journals and newspapers overseas (including *Foreign Affairs*, the *National Interest*, the *New York Times* and the *Wall Street Journal*). He has also addressed many major international conferences, including Davos, Williamsburg, Ditchley and the IISS meeting. These intellectual pursuits are a result of personal interest, not official duties.

By profession, Mr Mahbubani is a civil servant and career diplomat who has been with the Singapore Foreign Service since 1971. His overseas postings have included Cambodia (where he served during the war, in 1973–74), Malaysia, the United States and the United Nations. Currently, he is Permanent Secretary (Policy) at the Ministry of Foreign Affairs. He was the first dean of the Civil Service College in Singapore. He has served on the boards of several leading institutes and think tanks in Singapore, including the Institute of Southeast Asian Studies, the Institute of Policy Studies, the Lee Kuan Yew Exchange Fellowship and the Institute of Defence and Strategic Studies.

Mr Mahbubani was awarded the President's Scholarship in 1967, which enabled him to pursue undergraduate studies in philosophy at the University of Singapore (now the National University of Singapore). In 1976 he obtained a Master's degree, also in philosophy, from Dalhousie University in Canada, which also awarded him an honorary doctorate in 1995. He was a fellow at the Center for International Affairs at Harvard University in 1991–92.

Mr Mahbubani leaves shortly for New York, to resume his post of ambassador to the United Nations.